TUSCANY

The most beautiful region in Italy
nature, history, art

EDITION

officina
grafica
bolognese S.R.L.

TUSCANY

An outline of the history of Tuscany

From very ancient times, Tuscany has always been inhabited because of its beautiful bays and rock precipices overlooking the see, the lovely thick pine-forests, the sweet hills with their tall cypress trees, the mountains full of minerals and the temperate mediterranean climate.

The Etruscans were the population who left the deepest trace of their civilization. Although their history was wrapped in mystery, the historic reconstructions and the uncountable escavations have discovered tombs and towns which help us identify the first signs of their existence around year 1000 bC.

Unfortunately there are no precise indications about their writing and their language, nor about their origins. Some signs make us believe that they may have come from the cold nordic areas, others from Greece or from the neighbouring regions; others, finally, let us understand that they could be natives of the areas they lived in, that is to say in some parts of Emilia, in the whole of Tuscany, Umbria, Latium, Campania as well as on the Isle of Elba and Corsica.

The Etruscans did not found a real unitary State but they organized themselves into twelve cities (therefore called Dodecapolis) modelled on the Greek *polis*, which were linked to one-another by religious and cultural bonds; these ties, though, did not stop the different towns from fighting for the supremacy of the territory, especially in the areas full of mines. In fact, the Etruscans were the first to fuse and process metals. Magnificent vases, weapons, working tools, objects for the house and for female ornament were found in this area.

This proud people reached its maximum power in the 7th and 6th century bC when they expanded their hegemony both to the north and to the south, governing Rome for over 100 years. In the 5th century bC a slow but relentless decadence started, in that the Etruscans had to fight on all fronts to defend themselves from the attacks of the Greeks, the Carthaginians and the Romans who, between the 4th and the 3rd century bC, conquered all of Etruria transforming it into the 7th Region of the Empire.

Acknowledging the Etruscans' degree of civilization, the Romans left them a certain administrative, cultural and religious autonomy and at the same time tried to attain information about the processing of metals, the systems of fortification and the organization of life. The Roman Empire and later also Tuscany reached their maximum splendour in the centuries before the birth of Christ; in the following centuries they started to undergo a moral, political, religious and cultural decadence, allowing the nordic Barbarians to conquer all the territories which had been at the centre of the Roman dominion.

The region was first conquered by the Goths and by the Alemans, then by the Longobards in the 6th century AD. It was then annexed to the Marquisate of Tuscany and it managed to keep a slight cultural and religious unity between the different Free Cities and small States in which it was divided.

In the 12th and 13th century the Region was dominated by the Republic of Pisa, and in the 15th century it passed under the hegemony of Florence which in the meantime had become the real Capital thanks to the wise and far-sighted policy started by the Medici family; the Medicis transformed Florence into a very important cultural and artistic centre, setting the bases for the Renaissance. In these years the Medicis were the mecenates of two artistic geniusses of eternal and universal fame, namely Michelangelo Buonarroti and Leonardo da Vinci who are still a world-wide boast for Italy and especially for Tuscany.

Tuscany was the birthplace of many other artists and geniusses, who are still remembered for their Works. Among these were Dante, Boccaccio, Giotto, Galileo and Puccini, who are only some of the names of the many who have left behind masterpieces in every field of art. It would, in fact, take too long in this brief outline of history to quote the names of all the other artists who contributed to make Tuscany the most important cradle of art in all its forms.

In 1737 the last of the Medicis, Giangastone, handed the Grand Duchy over to the Lorenas who continued the Medici policy until when, around the end of the century, it was annexed to te French Empire after a large part of Italy had been conquered by Napoleon. Tuscany was then annexed to the Kingdom of Italy in 1860 and Florence became the Capital from 1865 to 1871.

1. typical Tuscan landscape
2. Gulf of Baratti
3. the map of the region
● : places of our itinerary

1

2

Castelnuovo di Garfagnana

Carrara

Barga

Massa

Bagni di Lucca

Marina di Carrara
Marina di Massa

Forte dei Marmi

Collodi

Pistoia

Viareggio

Pescia

Montecatini T.

Prato

Lucca

Vinci

Fiesole

Torre del Lago

Arno

Firenze

Pisa

Livorno

ISOLA DI GORGONA

San Gimignano

Poggibonsi

Arezzo

Castiglioncello

Volterra

Monteriggioni

Cortona

Marina di Cecina

Cecina

Siena

San Galgano

Castagneto Carducci

PARCO ARCHEOLOGICO
MINERARIO S. SILVESTRO

Montepulciano

ISOLA DI CAPRAIA

Campiglia Marittima

Massa Marittima

Ombrone

Pienza

Populonia - Baratti

Chianciano T.

PARCO DELLA MAREMMA

Porto Ferraio

Piombino

Roselle

Marciano Marina

Punta Ala

Porto Azzurro

Castiglione della Pescaia

Grosseto

Saturnia

Pitigliano

ISOLA D'ELBA

Magliano

Talamone

Porto S. Stefano

Orbetello
Ansedonia

ISOLA DEL GIGLIO

ISOLA DI MONTECRISTO

Porto Ercole

ISOLA DI GIANNUTRI

3

FLORENCE

Located in the valley of the Arno river which flows under its magnificent bridges and between the lovely palaces looking onto its banks, Florence is universally recognized as one of the most beautiful cities in the world, the seat of masterpieces of every kind.

Even in Florence and in its surroundings we find traces of the Etruscan and Roman civilizations, but the main historical features were set during the Late and (most of all) Early Middle Ages. Walking down the streets and the squares of the city centre feels like going back in time.

Still today the Guelfi and the Ghibellini families are used to indi-cate two factions fiercely fighting against each other. This is in fact what used to happen in the first centuries of the second mil-lenium when Florence (the capital of the Marquisate of Tuscany) lived through internal wars between the Ghibellinis, who were in favour of the Emperor, and the Guelfis, who were the representa-tives of the important tradesman and artisan association in favour of the coming of Florence under the Pope.

These fratricide battles have been described by Dante Alighieri, the great poet who lived in those dark years.

In spite of these terrible conflicts, the arts flourished and during the 13th and the 14th century Florence, which had by then expanded its dominion even over Arezzo, Pistoia and Siena, was the cradle for artists such as the above mentioned Dante, Cimabue and his pupil Giotto, and later Petrarca and Boccaccio.

Towards the end of the 14th century, after the riot of the Ciompi (i.e. Florentine wool-carder) in which the people uprised against the dominant class of the *Magnati*, the Seignory of the Medicis started: they governed Florence and other towns for almost three centuries, leaving indelible traces of their political, artistic and cultural far-sightedness. During the 15th century the Seignory of the Medicis reached its highest splendour with Lorenzo the Magnificent who brought artists such as Brunelleschi, Masaccio, Beato Angelico, Filippo Lippi, Botticelli, Donatello and others to his court to lay the bases of Renaissance, which reached its peak with Leonardo and Michelangelo.

The Seignory of the Medicis finished in 1737, so Florence came under the rule of the Grand Dukes of Lorena until 1865, when it was annexed to the Kingdom of Italy and became its Capital in 1871.

All the above mentioned artists have left traces of their Works in the fields of painting, sculpture and architecture, which still today make Florence a world-known centre of culture and the destination of an élite tourism which comes to admire the incomparable works kept in the squares, streets, churches, museums and theatres of this wonderful town.

Above: night view of the town
In the next pages: aerial view

5

THE CATHEDRAL

The Cathedral was built near the existing Baptistery and covered with polychromatic marble similar to the one used for the Baptistery itself. The building was started by Arnolfo di Cambio in 1296 on the ruins of the Cathedral of Santa Reparata. When the architect died in 1310, the work was interrupted and started again in 1357 under the direction of Francesco Talenti who enlarged its proportions, but then again it was left incomplete. It was not until 1436 that it was finished by Brunelleschi who studied its grand dome.

The original façade was demolished in 1587 and the most precious statues which decorated it were taken to the Museum of the Cathedral. The reasons for this demolition are still unknown. The rebuilding of it as we see it today was completed in 1887 under the direction of the architect De Fabris. In spite of the accuracy used to rebuild the façade four centuries later, we can see that its style is different compared to the apses and the side walls, that are still in their original version. The three bronze doors, most of the mosaic decorations and some of the statues were made between the last years of the 19th century and the first years of the 20th.

Walking around the outer perimetre of the Cathedral, starting from the left side, we come to *Porta della Balla* and then to *Porta della Mandorla (i.e. Portal of the Almond)* which is the most important for its decorations. On the fronton we see a high-relief, attributed to Manni di Bianco, of Our Lady enclosed in an almond. In the lunette is a splendid mosaic by Ghirlandaio,

1-2-3. aerial views of the monumental complex in Piazza Duomo

3

whereas on the sides, on the pinnacles, are two small statues of the Prophets, attributed to Donatello. Walking around the very large apse and stands sustaining the enormous dome by Brunelleschi, we come to the *Porta dei Canonici* first and them to the *Porta del Campanile (i.e. Bell-Tower Portal)*.

Inside the Cathedral we can admire the grandness of the pointed vaults and the arches dividing the three aisles and we are immediately attracted by the grandness of the octagonal apse overhung by Brunelleschi's dome, decorated with beautiful frescos by Vasari and Federico Zuccari and by lovely glass windows designed by Donatello. At the centre of the apse lies the choir and the main altar by Baccio Bandinelli and Giovanni Bandini; over the altar hangs a magnificent crucifix attributed to Benedetto da Maiano. From the apse we can enter into the two vestries: to the right is the old one, with its portal surmounted by a lunette containing a terracotta sculpture by Luca della Robbia; to the left is the new one, closed in a bronze door, famous because Lorenzo the Magnificent took refuge here during the *Congiura dei Pazzi* in 1478. Going back to the main entrance we can admire the magnificent glass windows by Ghiberti whereas in the Chapels of the side aisles are masterpieces by many other artists.

Outside, to the left, we see Giotto's Bell-Tower in all its grandeur; it was started in 1334 but after Giotto's death it was continued by Andrea Pisano first and by Francesco Talenti then, who completed it in 1359. It is almost 85 metres high and its square base is 14.45 metres big. The basement is decorated with copies of the lovely bas-reliefs now kept in the *Museum of the Cathedral*, whereas the three upper levels, by Talenti, are decorated with beautiful windows with two and three lights. All of the bell-tower is covered with polychromatic marble and decorated with terracottas and mosaics which make this Florentine Gothic architectural masterpiece unique in the world.

1. the Cathedral's façade
2. Giotto's Bell-tower
3. view from the roofs
4. inside the Cathedral
5. the Cathedral's central door

3

4

5

THE BAPTISTERY

It has an octagonal plan and it was built on the ruins of an existing Palaeochristian temple dating back to the 4th-5th century, as can be deducted from the ruins found in the foundations. It is dedicated to Saint John the Baptist, Patron saint of the town, and it was used as a Cathedral until 1128. The first rebuilding occurred during the 11th century and was completed, as we see it today, at the end of the 14th century.

The outer side is decorated with coloured marble and is characterized by three magnificent doors by Andrea Pisano and Lorenzo Ghiberti. The most famous is the *Porta est (i.e. East Door)*, which Michelangelo called *Porta del Paradiso (i.e. Heaven's Door)*. It was made between 1425 and 1452 by Ghiberti with the help of other artists, among which we remember Benozzo Gozzoli and Michelozzo. The ten beautiful panels forming it represent scenes from the Old Testament, whereas the side fillets represent Prophets and Sibyls alternated with figures of artists of the time, among which Ghiberti also placed himself. The upper part is decorated by a lovely group in marble by Andrea Sansovino whereas on the sides are two columns donated to Florence by the town of Pisa in 1117 to thank for its help in fighting the Saracens. This door was made by Ghiberti after many years spent in his laboratory and it condenses the style and the experience of a lifetime dedicated to sculpture.

The *Porta nord (i.e. North Door)* was made by Ghiberti in his youth (1403-1424) after having won a competition against the most important artists of the moment. At first sight we notice the different sensitiveness of the artist who was then still a novice, compared to his maturity which can be noticed in the *Porta del Paradiso*. It is made of 28 panels, 20 of which (the upper ones) represent scenes from the New Testament, whereas in the lower 8 are the Evangelists and the Doctors of the Church. In the upper part is the bronze group by Francesco Rustici representing Saint John the Baptist between the Leviathan and the Pharisee.

Finally, we come to the third door, the most ancient, made in 1330 by Andrea Pisano. This too is divided into 28 panels, of which the top 20 represent scenes from the life of Saint John the Baptist, whereas the lower 8 represent the Cardinal and Theological Virtues.

The Baptistery and the Loggia del Bigallo to the left, seen from Via Calzaioli

Inside the Baptistery we immediately notice the inlaid floor with signs of the Zodiac and oriental style drawings; the baptismal font from the Pisan school is also very nice. Along the right wall of the apse we can admire a lovely wooden statue and the grave of the anti-pope John 23rd, made by Donatello. The apses and the cupola are decorated with lovely mosaics made by Florentine and Venetian artists; they represent the history of the Genesis, with the *Creation of the World* and the *Last Judgement*. The large Christ placed in a non-central position is also very beautiful. It is a real triumph of mosaics which reminds us of the ones in Ravenna and in Venice for their Byzantine motives.

1. the east door, called Porta del Paradiso (i.e. Heaven's Door)

2. inside

3. the Byzantine mosaics in the dome

13

1

THE MUSEUM OF THE CATHEDRAL

The Museum of the Cathedral bears this name because it contains works of art deriving from the Cathedral, the Baptistery and the Bell-Tower. On the ground floor are some precious works by Arnolfo di Cambio (*Madonna with Child, Nativity Madonna and Boniface VIII*), Nanni di Banco's *San Luca* and Donatello's *San Giovanni*. On the first floor are two lovely Choirs by Donatello and Luca della Robbia and the 16 statues from the Bell-Tower. In the halls to the left and the right are the panel from the Bell-Tower, the famous *Altare del Battistero (i.e.Baptistery Altar)*, a beautiful work of jewellery, the *Deposizione (i.e. Deposition)* by Michelangelo, the *Annunziata (i.e. Virgin Mary)* and the *Arcangelo Gabriele (i.e. Archangel Gabriel)* by Jacopo della Quercia as well as many other paintings and sculptures.

1. the Altar, all made of silver, from the Baptistery, is a Gothic style masterpiece. The central statue was made by Michelozzo

2. Michelangelo: the "Deposition"

3. enamelled terracotta panel, from Giotto's Bell-tower, made by Alberto Arnoldi and representing the Eucharist.

2

3

THE CHURCH OF ORSANMICHELE

The name of this Church derives from that of *San Michele in Orto* to whom the existing building was devoted; the original church was demolished in 1284 to create a loggia used for trading corn. The building we see today was started in 1290 by Arnolfo di Cambio, but Francesco Talenti changed it in 1337 and other artists completed it in 1404. This building represents one of the most beautiful examples of the Florentine Gothic style, with its finely decorated portals and windows with two lights. The inside, divided into two aisles, is rectangular and at the end of the right aisle is the lovely *Tabernacle* by Andrea Orcagna. Even the main altar and the glass windows are beautiful. Next to the Church, connected by an elevated corridor, is the *Palazzo dell'Arte della Lana (i.e. Palace of the Art of Wool)*, built in the 14th century and composed of a *Casa Torre (i.e. Tower House)* which today is the seat of the *Società Dantesca (i.e. Dante Society)*.

1. façade of the Church and, to the right, the Palace of the Art of Wool

2. inside, the Tabernacle of the Orcagna

PIAZZA DELLA SIGNORIA

Dominated by the imposing vastness of the *Palazzo Vecchio*, surrounded by the beautiful *Loggia dei Lanzi* and by other lovely palaces, this splendid piazza was created between the 13th and the 14th century, after the houses of the most important Florentine families of the Ghibellini faction were demolished.

To the left of the *Palazzo Vecchio* is the *Fontana del Nettuno (i.e. Neptune Fountain)* also called *Fontana del Biancone*; it is an imposing sculpture made between 1563 and 1575 by Bartolomeo Ammannati and commissioned by Cosimo I de' Medici. Even the bronze statues representing river allegories with fauns and nynphs, placed in the corners of the basin and at the feet of the statue of Neptune are most attractive.

Opposite the fountain is a marble circle to reminds us of the place where Girolamo Savonarola was burnt on the stake on May 23rd, 1498.

Left of the fountain is Giambologna's equestrian statue of Cosimo I de' Medici. This square is where many demonstrations take place every year; among these are the *Gioco del Pallone (i.e. Ball Game)* in 16th century costumes and the *Mostra dei Fiori (i.e. Flower Exhibition)* during the *Maggio Fiorentino*.

1. Piazza della Signoria
2. the Neptune fountain, also called Biancone

THE LOGGIA DEI LANZI

The Loggia dei Lanzi was built between 1376 and 1391 by Benci di Cione and Simone Talenti in late Florentine Gothic style as the seat of the most important town events, among which were the election of the Priors and of the Gonfalonier. The name dei *Lanzi* derives from the fact that the Loggia was occupied by the Lansquenet army. Made of three large arches, it has elegant tiles above the pillars and two lions at the sides of the stairs.

1. aerial view
2. the Loggia dei Lanzi

PALAZZO VECCHIO

Palazzo Vecchio was built, starting in 1294, by Arnolfo di Cambio and was later enlarged even by Buontalenti and Vasari. Conceived to be the residence of the Priors, as a fortress-palace, it does in fact appear as a monolithic bloc, interrupted by two levels of elegant windows with two lights and an imposing crenellated terrace which is surmounted by the strong double-crenellated tower called *d'Arnolfo*.

As soon as we enter the Palazzo we find a nice courtyard surrounded by an elegant porch, which was restored by Michelozzo in 1453. At the centre of this courtyard is an elegant little fountain surmounted by a bronze putto created by Andrea del Verrocchio. An ample staircase designed by Vasari leads to the first floor where we find the lovely *Salone dei Cinquecento* by Cronaca, where the Main Town Council meets ever since the 16th century; from 1865 to 1871, when Florence was the Capital of the Kingdom of Italy, this was the seat of the Chamber of Deputies. The Town Council meets here since 1872. On the walls of this gorgeous hall are lovely paintings by Vasari's school and a lovely lacunar ceiling. On the right side, after having passed in front of Michelangelo's statues, we come to the *Studiolo di Francesco I*, then to the hall of the *Tesoretto di Cosimo I* (a secret writing-desk by Vasari) and finally to the *Sala dei Dugento* created in 1441 by Giuliano and Benedetto da Maiano.

On the second floor we find the *Quartiere degli Elementi* made by Battista del Tasso in 1550 and frescoed by Vasari.

1. the Courtyard by Michelozzo
2. the Salone dei Cinquecento

THE BARGELLO MUSEUM

Since 1859 the Bargello Museum has been the seat of the *Museo Nazionale (i.e. National Museum)* after having gone through a deep restoration to take this beautiful palace back to its original splendour. It was infact built in 1255 to be the seat of the *Capitanato del Popolo (i.e. Captaincy of the People)*. Its present name *Bargello* was established in 1574 when it became the seat of the *Capitano di Giustizia (i.e. Captain of Justice)* who was in fact called Bargello.

On the ground floor we find a magnificent entrance hall and a majestic courtyard. In the nearby halls we see numerous 14th century sculptures among which are some by Michelangelo, Cellini and Giambologna.

On the upper floor we find the *Salone di Donatello (i.e. Hall of Donatello)* which contains many works by the famous artist, as well as sculptures and panels by Luca della Robbia, Ghiberti and Brunelleschi.

1. the Palace of the Bargello seen from the lungarno

2. Michelangelo: Tondo Pitti

3. Luca della Robbia: Madonna of the rose-garden

4. in the two following pages: aerial view of the town

1

THE UFFIZI GALLERY

This lovely palace, placed between the Arno river and Piazza della Signoria, was built between 1560 and 1580 under the direction of the architect Giorgio Vasari; it was ordered by Cosimo I de' Medici to be used as the seat of administrative offices and as state archives.

In 1737 Anna Maria Ludovica de' Medici, the last member of the powerful family had the palace turned into a Museum and opened to the public; its 45 rooms, galleries and corridors contain very important works of art made by Italian and foreign artists, therefore this is the most complete and one of the most famous Italian museums in the world.

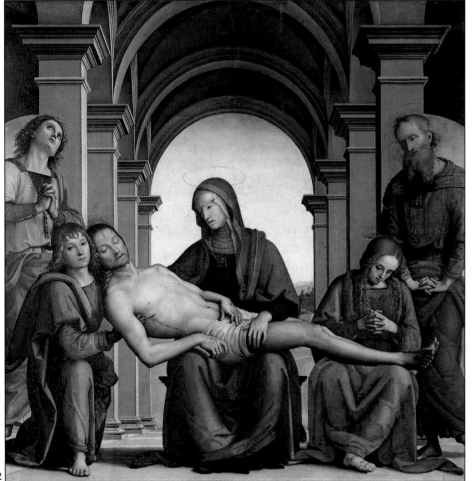

2

1. the courtyard of the Uffizi Gallery

2. Perugino: La Pietà

3. Sandro Botticelli:
La Primavera (i.e. Spring)

4. Sandro Botticelli: the birth of Venus

3

4

1

2

24

In the Uffizi we can see all the works from the Florentine and Tuscan schools, especially those dating back to the 15th century, which was the time of Florence's maximum splendour, but there are also many works from the Venetian and Flemish schools.

1. *Leonardo da Vinci: the Annunciation*
2. *Caravaggio: the sacrifice of Isaac*
3. *Michelangelo Buonarroti: the Holy Family*
4. *Tiziano: Flora*

25

PONTE VECCHIO

The Ponte Vecchio (i.e. Old Bridge) beares this name because it is for sure the most ancient bridge in town. It was first built in wood, then in the 12th century it was rebuilt in stone, but it was demolished by the fury of the waters during the terrible floods of 1333. In 1345 Neri di Fioravante started to rebuild it as we see it today with its typical *Botteghe (i.e. shops)* which were at first used only for food, but since the 16th century they have been used as laboratories for goldsmiths and silversmiths.

The shops are surmounted by the famous *Corridoio Vasariano (i.e. Vasari Corridor)* created by Vasari to allow Cosimo I de' Medici to go from Palazzo Vecchio to Palazzo Pitti without any risk.

1. the first corridor in the Uffizi Gallery

2-3. the Ponte Vecchio seen from upstream and from downstream

THE BASILICA OF SAN LORENZO

The Basilica of San Lorenzo is very old and was first consacrated by Saint Ambrose in 393. It was rebuilt in the 11th century in Pre-Romanesque style, then changed to look like we see it today by Filippo Brunelleschi in 1423. The façade is bare for the marble cover studied by Michelangelo was never made, for no precise reason. Inside, the three aisles are separated by Corinthian style columns. At the end of the central span are two lovely pulpits by Donatello. At the foot of the Main Altar is Cosimo I de' Medici's tomb, which is protected by metal grates.

At the end of the left transept we find the *Sacrestia Vecchia (i.e. Old Vestry)* by Brunelleschi who built it between 1419 and 1428, therefore before the Basilica was built.

1. the complex of the Basilica of San Lorenzo and the Medici Chapels with the typical market

2. Basilica of San Lorenzo: the Cloister

THE MEDICI CHAPELS AND THE NEW VESTRY

From the right transept of the Basilica of San Lorenzo we come to the *Sacrestia Nuova (i.e. New Vestry)* created by Michelangelo in 1520. There are many tombs and other works by this artist, so much so that all of the place oozes with Michelangelo's majestic grandeur.

From the apse, walking through a crypt by Buontalenti, where some members of the Medici family are buried, we come to the *Cappelle Medicee (i.e. Medici Chapels)* or dei *Principi (i.e. of the Princes)*.

This is an octagonal Baroque building with a very high dome, whose building was started in 1604 by the architect Nigetti, on a design by Giovanni de' Medici, revised and corrected by Buontalenti. On the walls of the vast hall decorated with polychromatic marble, are six large sarcophaguses and two big bronze statues by Ferdinando Tacca.

1. the Medici Chapels
2. Sepulchral chapel of the Medici princes
3. the New Vestry by Michelangelo

28

SANTA MARIA NOVELLA

The building of the church of Santa Maria Novella, which is a real jewel of the Florentine Gothic style, was started in 1246 by the Dominican friars Sisto da Firenze and Ristoro da Campi, and completed by Jacopo Talenti in about 1360.

The church is placed on the north side of a large pentagonal square where there are two obelisks by Giambologna which sided the way of the *Palio dei Cocchi*.

Its magnificent façade, started around 1300, was remade between 1456 and 1470 by Leon Battista Alberti who designed and built the portal and the upper part, characterized by inlays and heraldic sails by the Rucellais.

The inside, which is divided into three aisles, has polystyle columns sustaining pointed vaults. In the side aisles we find many chaples, all beautifully frescoed by famous maestros such as Giotto, Masaccio, Filippino Lippi and Ghirlandaio. The pulpit created by Brunelleschi on the second pillar is beautiful too. From the gate on the left hand side of the portal we come to the Cloisters of the great convent; among these we recall the first, called *Cappellone degli Spagnoli* which was built by Jacopo Talenti and frescoed by Andrea Bonaiuti.

1. the monumental complex of the Church of Santa Maria Novella

2. Domenico Ghirlandaio: the Angel's announcement to Zachariah (Main Chapel - detail)

1

THE ACCADEMIA GALLERY

Placed along the loggia of the *Galleria delle Belle Arti (i.e. Fine Arts Gallery)*, the Accademia Gallery contains many works by Michelangelo. Beyond the hall decorated with Flemish tapestries representing the Genesis, we come to the corridor leading to the apse.

Here are four *Prigioni (slaves)*, incomplete works destined to the tomb of Julius II in Saint Peter in Rome, as well as the *Pietà da Palestrina,* whose realization is not for sure attributed to Buonarroti.

At the centre of the Apse is the original version of the sculpture of *David* made by Michelangelo in his youth between 1501 and 1504. This masterpiece was initially placed at the entrance of *Palazzo Vecchio* where today we only see a copy.

In a hall at the side of the Apse is *Il Ratto delle Sabine (i.e. the Rape of the Sabines)*, a marble group by Giambologna previously placed in the *Loggia dei Lanzi.*

1. Michelangelo: "Pietà di Palestrina"
2. Michelangelo: one of the slaves
3. Michelangelo: detail of the hand of David
4. Michelangelo: "David"

2

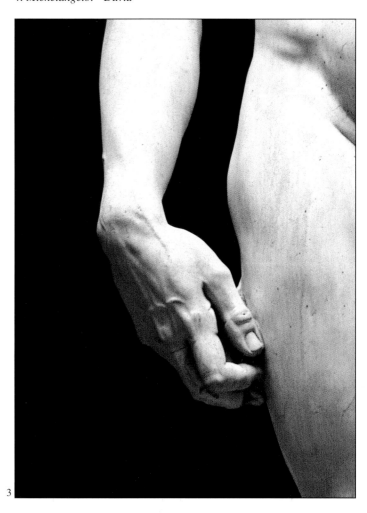

3

THE CHURCH AND CONVENT OF SAN MARCO

The building of the Church and Convent of San Marco was started at the end of the 13th century by the Silvestrini monks on the ruins of an oratory. Between 1437 and 1452 they were restored and enlarged by Michelozzo on Cosimo il Vecchio's commission. The Church was further restored by Giambologna towards 1580 and in the late 18th century by Silvani, whereas the Convent still bears its original Renaissance appearance. Among others, Beato Angelico, Savonarola and Fra Bartolomeo stayed here for some time.

From 1869 it has been the seat of the *Museo dell'Angelico (i.e. Beato Angelico Museum)*; Beato Angelico in fact lived here for some years, and left many works, the most important of which is the *Annunciazione (i.e. Annunciation)*, which we find on the first floor together with the beautiful library looked after by Michelozzo.

1. *Piazza and Church of San Marco*
2. *Beato Angelico: "the Deposition"*
3. *Domenico Ghirlandaio: "the Last Supper"*

THE ARCHAEOLOGICAL MUSEUM

The Archaeological Museum is full of works of art dating back to the Egyptian, the Etruscan and the Greek-Roman Civilizations. The *Vase collection* from all the different historic periods, the *Pre-historic section* and the *Middle-East section* are beautiful too. The *Etruscan section* is undoubtedly the richest, for it contains ruins gathered all over Tuscany. Among these is the *Chimera*, a beautiful bronze statue representing a roaring lion whose tail ends in a snake's head. It was found in 1553 in the area around Arezzo and it probably dates back to the 5th century bC. On the lion's right paw are the engraved letters *TINSCVIL* which can be interpreted in many ways. Even a statue of *Minerva* was found near Arezzo.

Notice the 5th century bronze statue called *l'Idolino (i.e. the small Idol)* in the *Greek-Roman section*.

1. Archaeological Museum: the Chimera

2. Archaeological Museum: Minerva

1

2

33

THE BASILICA DI SANTA CROCE

The beautiful Basilica of Santa Croce, with its Neo-Gothic façade, was built on a project by Arnolfo di Cambio towards the end of the 13th century. The grand exterior, divided into three aisles, contains the funeral monuments to many important people among which we recall Michelangelo Buonarroti, Niccolò Macchiavelli, Galileo Galilei, Vittorio Alfieri, Gioacchino Rossini and Ugo Foscolo. The two side aisles contain various Chapels among which are the *Bardi Chapel* and the *Peruzzi Chapel* on the walls of which are some beautiful paintings by Giotto.

In the central nave, which is famous for its uncovered truss ceiling, we find a lovely stone Tabernacle by Donatello, the beautiful octagonal Pulpit by Benedetto da Maiano and the Main Altar surmounted by a gorgeous polyptich with Madonna and Saints by Niccolò Gerini.

1. the façade

2. the central nave

3. the Cloister

4. Giotto: polyptych devoted to the coronation of the Virgin (Altar in the Baroncelli chapel)

5. Giotto: the exequies of San Francesco, fresco in the Bardi Chapel

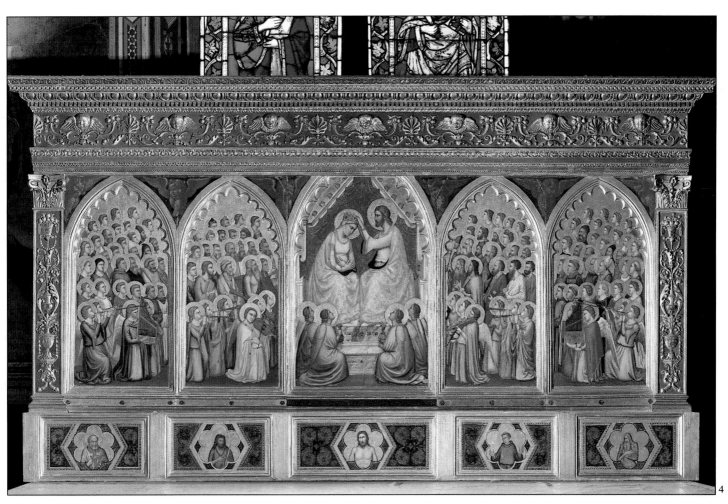

4

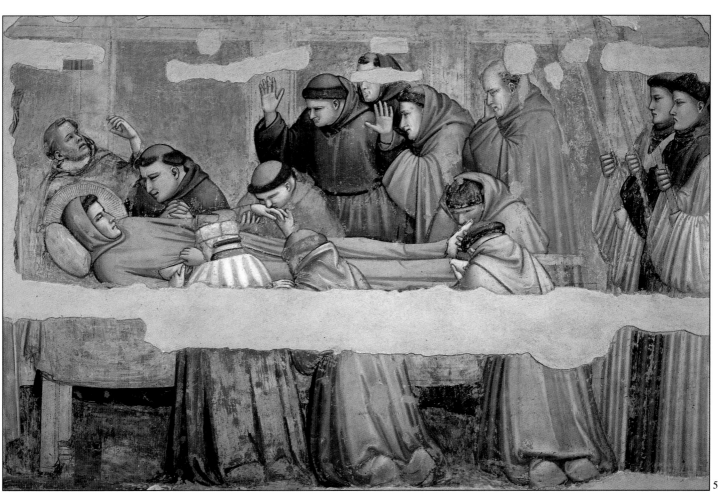

5

PALAZZO PITTI

The beautiful Palazzo Pitti lies at the foot of the Boboli hill and behind it are the lovely gardens bearing the same name. The building of this palace, which is one of the most imposing in town, was started in 1457 under the direction of the architect Luca Fancelli. The primitive project dated 1440 was assigned to Brunelleschi by the rich merchant Luca Pitti who at the time was a friend of the Medicis, the Lords of Florence; not long after that, they became enemies.

About a century later the property passed into the hands of the Medici family who decided to enlarge it, leaving the project and realization of the palace to Ammannati (1558). Other enlargements and the building of the two side wings were made in the following century.

From the main door we come to the magnificent courtyard designed by Ammannati, in which we notice Raffaele Curradi's *Grotta di Mosè (i.e. Moses' Grotto)*. On the right hand side is the Chapel containing a Crucifix by Giambologna and the *Scalone d'Onore (i.e. Honour Staircase)* which leads to the first floor where we find the *Quartieri Reali (i.e. Royal Quarters)* and the *Galleria Palatina (i.e. Palatinian Gallery)* ordered by Ferdinando II de' Medici. The Gallery, composed of many beautiful halls, is now the second museum in town and contains beautiful works of art by the main Italian artists.

Even the *Modern Art Gallery* and the *Museo delle Carrozze (i.e. Carriage Museum)* are remarkable.

The palace was lived in also by the Savoia family between 1865 and 1871, when Florence was the Capital of the Kingdom of Italy.

1. a splendid aerial view of Palazzo Pitti and the vast area in front of it. Behind it are the Boboli gardens and the Belvedere Fortress

2. Galleria Palatina: Halls of the Iliad

3. Guido Reni: Young Bacchus

4. Raffaello Sanzio: the Madonna of the Chair

2

3

4

1

THE BOBOLI GARDENS

2

Behind Palazzo Pitti, between the Belvedere fortress and Porta Romana, is this magnificent Italian garden that reaches practically over the entire hill.

Its realization started around the middle of the 16th century on a design by Niccolò Pericolo, called Tribolo, and was later enlarged by Ammannati and Buontalenti, who built a lovely artificial grotto, composed of many frescoed rooms.

As soon as we enter the gardens from the left side of the Palazzo Pitti we see the *Fontana del Bacchino (i.e. Fountain of the Small Bacchus)* representing Piero Barbino riding a tortoise (he was the dwarf at the court of Cosimo I de' Medici). Further on is an enormous basin called the *Vivaio di Nettuno (i.e. Neptune's Pond)* with a statue of the God of the Sea in the centre of it, created by Stoldo Lorenzi. Then we come to a small lake called *Piazzale dell'Isolotto* at the centre of which, on the isle, rises the gorgeous *Fontana del'Oceano (i.e. Ocean Fountain)* by Giambologna.

1. the Boboli Gardens: aerial view

2. the "Bacchino (i.e. Small Bacchus)" which is at the entrance of the Pitti Palace

FORTE DI BELVEDERE

Forte Belvedere, which today is the seat of important exhibitions and events, is made of strong perimetral ramparts surrounding a lovely small building. It is placed on the top of a hill from which the town is dominated and from which we can see a fantastic view.

It was built between 1590 and 1595 by Bernardo Buontalenti when Ferdinando I de' Medici commissioned it in order to better sight the enemies and defend the Pitti Palace, which at the time was the family residence.

1. the Belvedere Fortress: aerial view
2. the Boboli Gardens: the main avenue

PIAZZALE MICHELANGELO

Piazzale Michelangelo is placed on a hill from which we see a beautiful view of the town and it is dominated by an imposing statue of David placed in the centre of a sculptural group representing many of Buonarroti's works. It was built in 1868 on a design by the architect Giuseppe Poggi.

1. Piazzale Michelangelo: aerial view of the square and of Florence

2. detail of the "David": copy of Michelangelo's original

THE CHURCH OF SAN MINIATO AL MONTE

The building of this lovely church in Florentine Romanesque style was started in the first years of the 12th century and only finished in the last years of the 13th century. It is located at the top of a hill called *Monte delle Croci (i.e. Mountain of the Crosses)* and from its churchyard we can see a fantastic view of the town and its surroundings.

The lower part the façade is divided into five arches, whereas the upper part it contains a lovely mosaic representing *Cristo fra la Madonna e San Miniato (i.e. Christ between the Madonna and Saint Miniato)*.

Inside the church is divided into three aisles by polystyle colums; above our heads is an uncovered truss ceiling. See the beautiful Crypt on which rises the three nave Presbytery, in which we find a nice *Pergamo (i.e. Pulpit)*. Above the simple Main Altar we see a nice Crucifix attributed to Luca della Robbia. Even the Vestry is beautiful, with its frescoes by Spinello Aretino representing the *Storie della Leggenda di San Benedetto (i.e. Stories of the Legend of Saint Benedict)*.

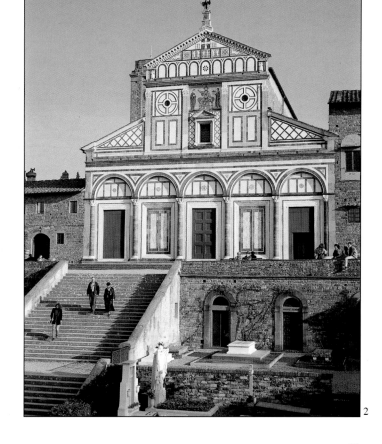

Church of San Miniato al Monte

1. aerial view of the whole monumental complex

2. the façade

THE CHARTREUSE OF GALLUZZO

The Chartreuse of Galluzzo is a vast complex of 14th century buildings ordered by Cardinal Niccolò Acciaiuoli whose body is buried here together with that of Cardinal Agnolo II in the Gothic style *Church of Santa Maria*, which is part of the Chartreuse.

To enter the complex we walk down a road enclosed between high walls; this leads to a porch at the entrance of the *Church of San Lorenzo* which is divided into two parts: the *Coro dei Conversi (i.e. Choir of the Lay Brothers)* and the *Coro dei Monaci (i.e. Choir of the Monks)*.

See the beautiful *Presbitery*. We then come to the vast *Chiostro Grande (i.e. Large Cloister)* built at the beginning of the 16th century, all surrounded by busts of Sybils, Prophets, Saints and two statues representing Adam and Eve. Notice the beautiful central well. There are two more cloisters enclosed in the series of vast buildings.

Aerial view

VILLA BERENSON

Villa Berenson is the seat of the American Harvard University in Italy. It is immersed in the green Tuscan hills and has a vast park and lovely gardens.

It contains a rich collection of works from the Italian Renaissance.

Aerial view

FIESOLE

Placed on a hill overlooking Florence, Fiesole is an ancient Etruscan town which later became an important Roman centre.

The centre of Fiesole is *Piazza Mino da Fiesole* with its beautiful 11th century *Cathedral of San Romolo* in which we see the *Cappella Salutati (i.e. Salutati Chapel)* frescoed by Cosimo Roselli, as well as the *Tomba del Vescovo Leonardo Salutati (i.e. Bishop Leonardo Salutati's Tomb)* by Mino da Fiesole. Opposite the Cathedral is the 11th century *Palazzo Vescovile (i.e. Bishop's Palace)* and the *Chiesa di Santa Maria Primerana (i.e. Church of Santa Maria Primerana)*. Walking up a steep road we come to the beautiful 14th century *Chiesa Convento di San Francesco (i.e. Convent Church of San Francesco)* with its *Museo Etnografico delle Missioni (i.e. Ethnographic Museum of the Missions)*.

From the square we easily come to the 1st century *Teatro Romano (i.e. Roman Theatre)* overlooking a most beautiful valley. The Theatre is well preserved and still today it hosts important theatre events. In the archeological sight annexed to it we find ruins of the ancient *Terme (i.e. Thermal Baths)*, the *Museo Civico (i.e. Municipal Museum)* with its numerous Etruscan and Roman ruins, and the ruins of an *Etruscan-Roman Temple*.

1. panoramic view coming from Florence

2. aerial view of the Roman Theatre and of Piazza Mino da Fiesole

3. Church of San Francesco

CERTALDO

Certaldo is famous for being the town where Giovanni Boccaccio was born (1313-1373). In the street bearing his name is still the house he was born in, which today is the seat of the *Centro Nazionale di Studi sul Boccaccio (i.e. National Centre of Studies on Boccaccio)*. In the historic centre rises the *Palazzo Pretorio o del Vicariato (i.e. Praetorial or Vicariate Palace)*, so called because it was the seat of the Vicari Fiorentini. The ancient part of town, called *Il Castello (i.e. The Castle)*, is till surrounded by ancient walls.

1. panoramic view
2. portrait of Boccaccio
3. the Praetorial Palace

PRATO

Placed between Florence and Pistoia at the foot of the *Monti della Calvana* and near the river Bisenzio, Prato (which has recently become a province) is an important centre, especially for its textile industry. Its origins are very old and in the city centre we can see the most beautiful 12th century Romanesque Cathedral of Santo Stefano. Outside, Donatello's *Pergamo del Sacro Cingolo (i.e. Pulpit of the Sacred Cincture)* stands out for its elegance. Inside is a very severe but beautiful Pulpit created by Mino da Fiesole with Rossellino. The walls were frescoed by Paolo Uccello, Filippo Lippi and others.

On Piazza del Duomo also rises the *Palazzo Vescovile (i.e. Bishop's Palace)* containing the *Museo dell'Opera del Duomo (i.e. Museum of the Cathedral)* in which we can see the works of the most important Tuscan artists.

The beautiful *Palazzo Comunale (i.e. Town-Hall)* and the *Palazzo Pretorio (i.e. Praetorial Palace)* contain the *Museo Civico (i.e. Municipal Museum)*. Nearby we can see the imposing *Castello dell'Imperatore (i.e. Emperor's Castle)* ordered by Frederick II of Swabia in the 13th century.

Worthy of notice are also the Churches of *San Francesco* and of *San Domenico*, both dating back to the 13th century, as well as the 15th century Church of *Santa Maria delle Carceri*.

1. aerial view

2. the Cathedral

3. the Emperor's Castle

4. the Praetorial Palace

1

2

4

3

VINCI

Vinci owes its fame to Leonardo, who in 1452 was born in the nearby Anchiano, where we can still see his house.

The town of Vinci, on the slopes of Monte Albano, developes around the 13th century *Castello dei Conti Guidi (Castle of the Counts Guidi)*, where today rises the Museum devoted to the great genius, containing his drawings and writings, as well as the prototypes of the machines he studied.

On April 15th, the day of Leonardo's birth, important commemorative celebrations are held here every year.

1. the Castle of the Guidi Counts, seat of the Museum

2. the entrance to the library

3. Anchiano: the house where Leonardo was born

4. inside Leonardo's house

PISTOIA

Pistoia is a beautiful town reaching out into the plains of the Ombrone river, between the Arno and Monte Albano, at the foot of the Apennines.

The city centre, surrounded by the *Mura Medicee (i.e. Medici Walls)*, develops around the *Piazza del Duomo (i.e. Cathedral Square)* on which the most important city monuments rise: the most important is probably the *Cattedrale (i.e. Cathedral)* from the 12th-13th century with its elegant porch whose central vault is decorated with a bas-relief in enamelled terracotta by Andrea della Robbia. The Cathedral is divided into three aisles and contains many works of art. At the sides of this building there are the *Museo del Tesoro (i.e. Museum of the Treasure)* and the 11th century *Palazzo dei Vescovi (i.e. Bishops' Palace)* with its Gothic

1. aerial view
2. the Cathedral and the Bishops' Palace

1

2

style façade decorated with elegant windows with two lights and ogive windows. Opposite the Cathedral rises the *Battistero (i.e. Baptistery)*, an elegant building in Gothic style, with an octagonal plan, built between 1338 and 1359 by Cellino di Nese on a project by Andrea Pisano.

Next to the Baptistery, in the wider part of the square, rises the 14th century *Palazzo Pretorio (i.e. Praetorial Palace)*, which today is the Law-court, with its beautiful façade decorated with coats-of-arms and two orders of windows with two lights.

On the opposite side of the square rises the 13th century *Palazzo Comunale (i.e.Town-Hall)*, a severe building in sandstone, with lovely windows with two lights on the first floor and with three lights on the second floor, leaning on an porch with Gothic arches. The palace contains the *Museo Civico (i.e. Municipal Museum)*.

Other buildings worthy of notice are the *Ospedale del Ceppo* on whose façade above the elegant porch we see some very precious enamelled terracottas from the school of Andrea della Robbia; then the 12th century *Palazzo dei Capitani del Popolo (i.e. Palace of the Captains of the People)*, the *Fortezza Medicea (i.e. Medici Fortress)* and the Churches of *San Giovanni Fuoricivitas* in Roma-nesque style, of *San Francesco* in Gothic style, and of the *Madonna dell'Umiltà* in Renaissance style.

1. the Town-hall

2. the Praetorial Palace

3. the Ceppo Hospital with its enamelled terracotta reliefs

4. the Baptistery

3

4

MONTECATINI TERME

Montecatini Terme is a pretty little town between Pistoia and Lucca at the foot of the charming Nievole Valley, and it is very well known for its thermal spas which rise around eight springs.

The Thermal baths were known in very ancient times, but the building of the main spas only started towards the end of the 18th century, therefore the look of Montecatini Terme is quite modern, with its well-kept gardens and wide avenues.

Behind the thermal town, on the slopes of a steep hill, rises *Montecatini Alto*, an evocative Medieval village with its artistically interesting ancient buildings.

1. aerial view
2. inside the Tettuccio thermal spa

MONTECATINI VAL DI NIEVOLE

This town, also known as *Montecatini Alto*, dominates the thermal town from the top of a hill. For its dominant position, it was the object of harsh quarrels between Lucca and Florence in the 13th and 14th century. The town, which is typically Medieval, is dominated by the Rocca (i.e. Fortress) surrounded by pentagonal walls. See the lovely *Church of San Pietro*, in Romanesque style, annexed to a museum, in which we can see vestments, vessels and paintings from the 16th and 17th century.

PESCIA

Pescia is a delightful small town renowned mainly for its great *Flower Market*, the biggest in the whole of Tuscany. In the past it was also a great centre for the production of special paper for the publishing trade and for the printing of banknotes.

Its historic centre is typically Medieval and so are the lovely *Cathedral* and *Palazzo Pretorio (i.e. Praetorial Palace)*.

1. Montecatini Alto: view
2. Pescia: Piazza Mazzini
3. the stream Pescia

COLLODI

Well-known especially for the *Parco di Pinocchio (i.e. Pinocchio's Park)*, Collodi is the favourite destination of many children who, by coming here and looking at all the monuments and mosaics, can relive the story of the famous puppet. Pinocchio was created by the writer Carlo Lorenzini (1826-1890), who decided to change his name into that of the town where he had spent his youth.

Collodi is a village of Medieval origin, dominated by an ancient Church placed behind the grand *Villa Garzoni*, which was built between 1633 and 1662 in Baroque-Lucchese style.

1. the Whale
2. the Cat and the Fox
3. Pinocchio and the Fairy
4. aerial view of the Park in Villa Garzoni

LUCCA

Lucca owes its birth to the Ligurians, Etruscans and Romans, although previous discoveries witness human settlements dating back to the Palaeolithic Era. Its name is most probably due to the Ligurian Celts, who called the place *Luck*, meaning *area of marshes*. Although the name dates back to that period (or so say the scholars), it was not until about the 3rd century bC that, thanks to the Romans, Lucca took on the aspect of an important centre, becoming a well-known Roman piazza (i.e. square). A bit longer than a century later, around 180 bC, it became a Latin colony and in '89 a Roman municipality. It is important to remember that the famous encounter between Caesar, Crasso and Pompey took place here in 56 bC.

But the most brilliant years occurred during the first two centuries of the Christian Era, of which there are some superlative evidences: a circle of walls, the Anfitheatre, etc.

Its arrangement in a strategic position has quite encouraged life here: not only do many roads such as the Clodia, the Aurelia and the Cassia wind around Lucca, but both the Goths and the Longobards considered it (and declared it) to be the capital town of Tuscia. Having converted to Catholicism, the latter divided this area into Dioceses with different Parishes, therefore giving rise to another period of the town's politic and economic splendour.

1. view of bell-towers and towers

2. aerial view: in the foreground the Walls and the Cathedral of San Martino

1. the Cathedral of San Martino
2. San Martino: detail of the sarcophagus of Ilaria del Carretto
3. aerial view of the Cathedral
4. the Labyrinth

But it was not until the First Crusade (which Lucca's inhabitants widely took part in) that the town further enlarged its prestige becoming a Commune, and in the 13th century its fame started to expand so much that it became a large centre of commerce not only with Europe but also with the East (it became famous especially for its silk).

And again it was in this period that the centre of Lucca was enriched with architectonic beauties (see the second circle of walls, many churches, etc.); even the houses were made to look more attractive and they started to be built in the shape of towers, often decorated with green tufts on the top.

At the same time, though, internal and sanguinary fights started between the feudal aristocracy and the *merchant* middle-classes (the Ghibellinis and the Guelfis) and then, when the latter won, between the Bianchis and the Neris. In the end, it was the Neris who prevailed, forever banishing the Antelminellis from town. But Lucca owes Castruccio Castracani, one of the most famous representatives of this family, one of the most brilliant moments of its history. The great leader, in fact, managed to extend the power of his town over great part of Tuscany. At his death, the town fights started again, therefore making Lucca a domain of its rival, Pisa.

From 1400 and for 30 years, Paolo Guinigi was Lord in Lucca; his power in those years is proved by numerous buildings, such as the Guinigi Palace, the homonymous villa and Jacopo della Quercia's sarcophagus in which lies Ilaria del Carretto, his young wife. At his fall, caused by Francesco Sforza's nobles, the republic of Lucca came across some difficult moments; the neighbouring Florence gained supremacy over the territory.

So the entire concept of life in the town changed: now people were aiming at self-defence (a new circle of walls was built to try and stop enemy attacks) and concentrating no longer on commerce, but on agriculture. In this period, the 16th century, many beautiful countryside villas, of which we can still see the remains today, were built.

With no great excitement, the republic of Lucca lived quietly until the end of the 18th century, when it was taken over by Napoleon's Empire. It was changed into a principality and assigned to Elisa Baciocchi, the Emperor's sister, until 1814; three years later it was annexed to the Granducato of Tuscany and then, together, they became part of the Italian Kingdom.

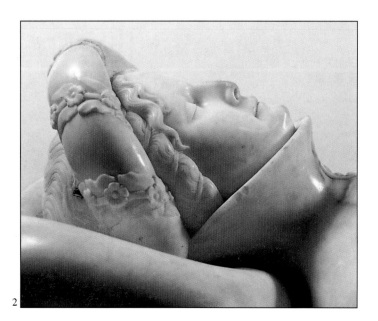

3

IL DUOMO

The Cathedral was built for the first time in the 6th century for order, it seems, of San Frediano; later it was rebuilt in the 11th century for order of the Bishop Anselmo da Baggio who consacrated it in 1070 at the presence of Matilde di Canossa. The Romanesque style version we see today is due to a further rebuilding and restorations in the 12th century.

The façade presents a porch with three arches, of which the one to the right is smaller than the others, and they are all surmounted by three orders of smaller arches. Before entering the building we meet the *Labyrinth*. The Gothic exterior is divided into three aisles, whose arches are finely decorated. In the aisles we can admire many works of art, among which we recall the *Sarcophagus of Ilaria del Carretto*, a lovely marble work made by Jacopo della Quercia in 1405; a magnificent *Last Supper* by Tintoretto; the lovely *Small Temple* with octagonal base by Matteo Cividali, inside which is the *Volto Santo (i.e. Holy Face)*, a wooden crucifix representing the Redeemer who, every year, in September, is dressed with rich vestments and taken in procession to remember the many miracles attributed to Him. See the beautiful organ *Choir*.

Leaving the Cathedral we can admire the 14th century *Baptistery* and the 12th century *Church of San Giovanni*.

4

1. "The Last Supper" by Tintoretto
2. detail of the arches between the aisles
3. the Holy Face

SAN FREDIANO

The beautiful Church of San Giovanni was built in the 12th century on the ruins of an existing Temple. Rebuilt and enlarged in the 12th and 14th century, its very severe façade is surmounted by a huge Byzantine style mosaic representing the *Ascension of Christ*. Inside there are three aisles and many works of art, among which is the sarcophagus containing the intact body of Saint Zita, the town's Patron Saint. See the beautiful Romanesque *Baptismal Font*.

1. the Baptismal Font

2. the façade

3. the Apse and the Bell-tower

1

2

3

1. the Guinigi Tower, placed on the homonymous palace, typical for the holm-oak growing on the top of it

2. Madonna dello Stellario by Giovanni Larroni, 1687

3. Via dei Fossi

4-5. Piazza dell'Anfiteatro, rebuilt in 1830 by the architect Lorenzo Nottolini on the rests of a Roman Anfitheatre from the 2nd century

4

5

SAN MICHELE IN FORO

Even the Church of San Michele in Foro was built in the 12th century and represents one of the few examples of Romanesque architecture in Pisan-Lucchese style.

Its façade has four orders of arches and is surmounted by the statue of Saint Michael. Inside there are three aisles and many works of art.

1. the monumental complex

2. the statue of San Michele at the top of the façade

3. Filippino Lippi (1457-1504): "San Rocco, San Sebastiano, San Gerolamo and Sant'Elena"

THE PALACES AND VILLAS

Palazzo Pfanner, formerly known as *Palazzo Contorni*, was built in the second half of the 17th century almost in the centre of town; its splendid garden contains an octagonal basin surrounded by statues.

Among the famous Lucchese Villas we recall *Villa Torriggiani di Camigliano* built in the 16th and 17th century, and *Villa Mansi* from the same period, in Secramigno. Both have lovely façades, sumptuous halls and splendid gardens with small lakes.

1. Palazzo Pfanner: the illuminated garden
2. Villa Torriggiani
3. Villa Mansi

61

THE GARFAGNANA AREA AND THE LIMA VALLEY

The Garfagnana area extends along most of the course of the Serchio river, flowing between the two chains of the Apuane Alps and of the Apennines; since these mountains are very different from one another, we can say that this territory has a unique landscape. This area lies in the northern part of Tuscany on the border to Luigiana and to the Emilia Apennine.

Although it was inhabited by Ligurians and Romans in very ancient times, Garfagnana gained historic importance only from the times of Matilde di Canossa; due to the division of the area among various Seignories in those days, in fact, new connections had to be established between Emilia and the Tyrrhenian Sea, in alternative to the plains.

The villages, the monasteries, the castles, the parishes and the bridges scattered all over the territory are typically Medieval and they are particularly attractive to the tourists, who in Garfagnana can satisfy their wish to live in nature and admire the work of man in the course of the centuries.

BORGO A MOZZANO

Coming from Lucca, along the Brennero state road, the first town we meet is Borgo a Mozzano, a typically Medieval village characterized by the *Ponte della Maddalena (i.e. Magdalene's Bridge)*, commonly known as the *Ponte del Diavolo (i.e. Devil's Bridge)* because the legend says it was built by the Evil in only one night. This ecceptional bridge, with its asymmetrical arches and its peculiar shape, was probably ordered by the Countess Matilde di Canossa and built during the 14th century.

BAGNI DI LUCCA

The charming town of Bagni di Lucca, made up of numerous fractions developing along the Lima river, is well-known for its Thermal baths, which were famous already in the 11th century. The town's greatest fame was reached at the beginning of the 19th century because this is where the Lucchese nobility used to invite all the European aristocrates as well as the most famous artists such as

Montaigne, Byron, Shelley, D'Azeglio and Carducci.

The success, even today, of the Thermal baths is due to the high temperature and the radioactivity of the water. Plunged in nature and surrounded by magnificent Luccese style villas, Bagni di Lucca is really a beautiful place to see.

BARGA

Placed at the top of a high hill, Barga is a lovely Medieval village dominated by its *Cathedral*. The city centre, surrounded by walls, is characterized by narrow and steep alleys along which rise beautiful buildings. In the Middle Ages Barga was famous for producing and trading silk.

The modern part of this small town is placed more towards the valley and is called *Il Giardino (i.e. The Garden).*

1. trekking

2. Borgo a Mozzano: the Devil's Bridge

3. Bagni di Lucca: view

4. Bagni di Lucca: Ponte a Serraglio on the Lima river

5. Barga: view, at the top, the Cathedral

6. Barga: the Cathedral (13th century)

CASTELVECCHIO PASCOLI

The small village of Castelvecchio Pascoli, which rises only a few km from Barga, owes its fame to the poet Giovanni Pascoli who used to spend long periods of time in his house, which today has become a Museum.

LE PANIE

Le Panie is one of the major massifs of the Apuane Alps and it is composed of three peaks: the *Punta della Croce*, the *Pania Secca* and the *Pizzo delle Saette*.

1. Castelvecchio Pascoli: portrait of the poet by Cordati, in Barga's Town Hall

2. Castelvecchio Pascoli: the poet's house

3. le Panie: Uomo Morto (i.e. the Dead Man)

CASTELNUOVO GARFAGNANA

Castelnuovo Garfagnana is the most important village in this area and the seat of the *Comunità Montana (i.e. Mountain Comunity)* made of 16 Municipalities. Placed at the confluence between the Turrite Secchia and the Serchio rivers, this small town has a Medieval structure and is dominated by the 12th century *Rocca Ariostesca (i.e. Fortress of Ariosto),* so called because the great poet Ludovico Ariosto stayed here when the Estensis were the Lords of Castelnuovo.

VAGLI DI SOTTO

Vagli di Sotto is a sweet little village enriched by the presence of the 12th century *Church of San Regolo,* dominating the large artificial basin in which another small village called Fabbriche was flooded; when the basin is drained, the hamlet comes to the surface.

1. The Arch in the Panie mountains

2. Castelnuovo G.: Rocca Ariostesca (i.e. Fortress of Ariosto)

3. Vagli di Sotto: the lake full of water

4. Vagli di Sotto: the drained lake with the remains of the old village

TORRE DEL LAGO

Torre del Lago is a small village between Lucca and Viareggio, which owes its fame to the great composer Giacomo Puccini, who built a pretty villa along the shores of the Massaciuccoli lake, where he composed most of his works. Today the villa has been turned into the *Museo Pucciniano (i.e. Puccini Museum)* with the Maestro's tomb in a hall used as Chapel.

Every year, in the summer, Torre del Lago hosts the open-air *Festival Pucciniano,* during which the musician's most important works are represented.

1-2. Aerial views of the lake of Massaciuccoli
3. Portrait of Giacomo Puccini

3

VIAREGGIO

Viareggio is Versilia's most popular seaside resort with its beautiful beach full of Italian and foreign tourists who also come here for Carnival to see the enormous carts parading through town.

Beautiful avenues lined with palmtrees, oleanders and Mediterranean plants run through the residential area placed between the grand Apuane Alps and the sea, in two huge pine-forests.

The very large port of Viareggio contains most of Tuscany's fishing flotilla and many shipyards in which boats are built and exported around the world.

What remains of the Medieval city is only the *Torre Matilde (i.e. Matilde Tower)* built in 1534 within a fortified system for the defence of the port.

The most important monuments in town date back to the end of the 19th-beginning of the 20th century; among these we recall the *Teatro Margherita (i.e. Margherita Theatre)*, the *Palazzo delle Muse (i.e. Palace of the Muses)*, the seat of the *A.C. Blanc Museum* and the *Bagno Balena.*

1. The promenade and the Margherita Theatre

2. The entrance to the port

3. The beach

4. Carnival

LIDO DI CAMAIORE

The beautiful and vast beach

MARINA DI PIETRASANTA

The beautiful and vast beach and the Apuane Alps in the background

CINQUALE DI MONTIGNOSO

The beautiful beach, the tourist port and the canal port

FORTE DEI MARMI

Forte dei Marmi owes its name to the fact that in ancient times it was the port from which the marbles from the nearby Apuane Alps took off, and also to the *Forte (i.e. Fortress)* ordered by Leopoldo I in 1788 to better defend the port.

Forte dei Marmi developed as a seaside resort towards the end of the 19th century and it still today is one of the favourite destinations of the refined and élite tourists, because there are many beautiful villas plunged in the vegetation of the enormous pine-forest surrounding this small town.

1. The beach and the Apuane Alps

2. The "Fortress"

3. The bathing establishments seen from the wharf

MASSA

Massa is made up of a Medieval centre rising on the slopes of the Apuane Alps, five km from the sea, dominated by the *Castello Malaspina (i.e. Malaspina Castle)* which belongs to a large fortified complex built between the 15th and the 16th century.

The most modern part of the town stretches to the sea and to the port. Among the most important town monuments we recall the 1557 *Palazzo Cybo Malaspina* which today is the seat of the Prefecture, the beautiful *Cathedral* and the annexed *Museo di Arte Sacra (i.e. Sacred Art Museum)*.

1. View of the hill with the fortress

2. Renaissance palace in the Malaspina Fortress

3. Palazzo Cybo Malaspina: the façade

4. Palazzo Cybo Malaspina: the inner courtyard

MARINA DI MASSA

On the border to the town of Massa to which it is connected by means of a very long avenue planted with trees, the town of Marina di Massa is an elegant seaside resort surrounded by pine-forests and defended by the grand Apuane Alps.

Provided with modern equipment, Marina di Massa offers all its tourists a good receptiveness and the possibility of spending a happy holiday.

1. View from the wharf

2. The beach and the seaside

3. Aerial view of the beach, the village and the Apuane Alps

4. Apuane Alps: a marble cave

CARRARA

Placed on the banks of the Carrione stream, Carrara is separated from Massa by the *Colline di Candia (i.e. Hills of Candia)*.

For over 2,000 years it has been the Capital of marble carved in the nearby Apuane Alps, so much so that Carrara is considered the seat of the *Museo del Marmo (i.e. Marble Museum)*. This material completely covers the "Cathedral" which was built between the 11th and the 13th century in Romanesque style. Even in Carrara, as well as in Massa, we find a contemporary *Palazzo Cybo Malaspina,* today the seat of the *Accademia delle Belle Arti (i.e. Fine Arts Academy)*. Do not forget to see *Piazza Alberica* with the *Fontana del Gigante (i.e. Giant's Fountain)* devoted to Andrea Doria.

1

2

MARINA DI CARRARA

Marina di Carrara is placed on the most extreme point of the Tyrrhenian coast of Tuscany, on the border to Liguria. This is where the marble extracted from the Apuane Alps is embarked. On the sides of the huge port limited by two piers are two beautiful beaches.

1. Carrara, Piazza Alberica with the Fountain of the Giant

2. Carrara, Palazzo Cybo, the seat of the Fine Arts Academy

3. Marina di Carrara, Aerial view of the port and the Apuane Alps

3

1

2

3

ANCIENT LUNI

The origins of Luni are controversial: some scholars consider it to be of Etruscan origin, whereas others attribute its founding to the Romans. The second hypothesis is the most credible, also because it is witnessed by many ruins of evident Roman origin which were found during recent escavations. It has been proved that in 177 bC Luni was a flourishing Roman colony devoted to trading marble from the nearby Apuane Alps. Luni's decadence started with malaria epidemics, and in the following centuries it became a victim of carried out by the Longobards, Normans and Saracens sacks and destructions.

Recent escavations have brought to the light the ruins of some buildings, walls, objects, tools, as well as a large anfitheatre from the 1st century which could contain 6,000 people.

In the Middle Ages Luni gave its name to the surrounding area called *Lunigiana*.

1-2: Views of the excavations with the Apuane Alps in the background

3. A hall in the Museum

4. The statue of the Acefala Loricata

5. Aerial view of the great Roman Anfitheatre

6. Aerial vew of the excavations

4

PISA

Only about ten km from the sea and four metres above its level, in a vast alluvial plain protected by Monte Pisano, rises the town of Pisa, divided in two by the Arno river.

Its origins are uncertain, but already the historian Livio spoke about it as the town founded by the Ligurians. It became a flourishing colony of the Empire after having been an ally of the Romans against the Carthaginians during the second *Punic War* in the 1st century bC.

In the 7th century AD Pisa passed under the Longobard rule and became an important port, for it was the only opening onto the sea. Having came under the *Marquisate of Tuscany,* though, at the beginning of the 11th century, it managed to become a *Free City*, therefore giving rise to the period in which Pisa had its greatest development. During the following three centuries, it became one of the greatest maritime powers of the Mediterranean. Pisa won almost all the naval battles against the fleets of the other Maritime Republics (Genoa and Amalfi first, Venice later), but in 1284 it lost the *Battaglia della Meloria* and so it started to fall.

In the 11th and 12th century, when Pisa took part in the first Crusade, the building of the monuments which make it still world-famous today was started. The arts flourished and thanks to the brilliant mind of Nicola Pisano, his son Giovanni and Arnolfo di Cambio, the first Schools started to be founded. They were the first centre of University, later further developed by Galileo Galilei who created a department for Mathematics and Physics, which is still today one of the most important in the world.

In the years between the 14th and the 19th century, the town was ruled by the Medici and the Lorena families who left traces of their political and cultural far-sightedness, by further increasing the Studio della Sapienza and the Scuola Normale Superiore.

In 1860, with a popular plebiscite, Pisa entered the Kingdom of Italy.

Today Pisa is the destination of considerable numbers of tourists who come to admire the gorgeous *Piazza dei Miracoli* which gathers all the monuments that make it so famous are gathered.

1. View from the roofs

2. Sunset on the Arno river towards the sea

3. The ancient Porta Nuova

4. In the next two pages: aerial view of Piazza dei Miracoli

3

THE CATHEDRAL

The building of this masterpiece of Romanesque-Pisan art started in 1063 under the direction of the architect Buschetto. The end of the works, and mainly the building of the façade as we see it today, occurred only two centuries later thanks to the work of the architect Rainaldo. Its shape is that of a Latin cross, with a huge apse and an imposing dome covering it.

The façade is characterized by five orders of arches and by three lovely bronze portals. The original portals were made by Bonanno, but they were destroyed in 1595 by a severe fire. The ones we see today were created by Francavilla, Mocchi and Tacca, who were part of Giambologna's school. On the panels of the central door are images from the life of Mary, whereas on the two side doors are scenes from the life of Jesus.

Inside, the five aisles are divided by tall columns with Corinthian capitals sustaining the *Matronei (i.e. Women's Corridors)* placed over the side aisles. Above our heads is the beautiful lacunar ceiling, whereas the ceiling over the great apse is decorated with a lovely mosaic representing *Christ on the Throne.*

Even the Pulpit created by Giovanni Pisano in the first years of the 14th century is beautiful: it lies against the first pillar to the left of the great dome and it has a hexagonal plan on a round base. The central column represents the *Art of the Trivium and Quadrivium,* whereas the other columns, some of which resting on lions, represent the *Four Cardinal Virtues* sustaining the Church, the *Evangelists* sustaining Christ, and other images of the period. The capitals are decorated with figures of Sibyls. The nine panels forming the parapet represent scenes which preceded and followed the birth of the Redeemer.

The Cathedral

1. The façade

2. The central portal

3. The façade, dome and apse

4. The door of San Ranieri

5. The door of San Ranieri: detail of the portal

3

4

5

1

3

2

1. *The apsal part seen from the pulpit; top right: Galileo's lamp*

2. *Women's corridor seen from a side chapel*

3. *The pulpit by Giovanni Pisano*

4. *The central aisle*

THE BAPTISTERY

The building of this grand monument, which is 55 metres tall and has a diametre of over 35 metres, started in 1153 under the direction of the architect Diotisalvi, but it was almost completed only a century later under the guidance of Nicola Pisano, for the works were interrupted various times because of various wars fought by the Republic. Only towards the end of the following century, under the direction of the architects Cellino di Nave and Zimbelino Bolognese were the works completed with the creation of very precious Gothic decorations which embellish the two upper levels of the external façade; on the contrary, the arch-

es surrounding the basement are much barer.

There are four entrance doors, the most important of which is the one facing the Cathedral. Inside the Baptistery, in the centre, is the imposing Baptismal Font, at the side of which we see the gorgeous Pulpit, engraved by Nicola Pisano in the 13th century during the second phase of the works.

1. *The Baptistery seen from the Cathedral*

2. *The Baptistery with the Cathedral and the Tower*

3. *The Baptismal Font and the Pulpit by Nicola Pisano*

4. *Aerial view of the monumental complex*

5. *The Baptismal Font seen from the Women's Corridor*

THE TOWER

The Hanging Tower of Pisa has been called *one of the world's seven wonders,* which is enough to give the idea of this really unique monument. The main particularity is its gradient, certainly due to a collapse of the ground occurred during its building in Romanesque style, which started in 1174 under the direction of Bonanno Pisano.

During the course of the centuries the Tower has continued to increase its gradient by about 1 mm a year, so much so that in these last few years it has been necessary to do something to stop it from falling. Reinforced concrete has been injected under the base of the hanging side whereas big steel tie-beems have been applied to the opposite side. The possible fall of the Tower would in fact be a huge catastrophe, in that, beyond losing one of the world's seven wonders we would also lose all the surrounding monuments.

The beautiful entrance door is surmounted by a lunette containing an image of a *Madonna with Child and Saint Peter and Saint John* by the sculptor Andrea Quadri. The basement is divided into large arches decorated with bas-reliefs. The intermediate part is divided into six loggias separated by corniches sustained by slim columns, each one with a differently decorated capital. The bell-

1. The Tower

2. Impressive aerial view of the Tower and of the monumental complex in Piazza dei Miracoli

1   2

cell is divided into a series of arches recalling the ones in the basement. The cell contains seven bells, each of which is tuned to a different note. The most ancient of all, the *Pasquereccia* is famous because it rang to announce that Count Ugolino della Gherardesca, accused of traison, was dying of hunger with all the members of his family. This episode has also been described by Dante in the *Divine Comedy*.

The Hanging Tower is famous even because from its top and thanks to its incline, Galileo Galilei, one of Pisa's most famous citizens, carried out some of his most important experiments concerning the gravitation of the bodies.

The Tower's maximum height is 56.70 m; the outer diametre of the base is 15.48 m, whereas the inner diametre is 7.37 m. The foundations are more than three metres deep and the maximum incline reached in our time is about 4.60 m.

1-2-3. Impressive views of the Hanging Tower from various positions

THE MUSEUM OF THE CATHEDRAL

The Museum of the Cathedral was organized in 1986 in the specially restored building called *Casa dei Canonici (i.e. House of the Canons)*. The museum develops in 23 halls, in the corridors which connect them and in the galleries of the magnificent Cloister from which we see a lovely view of the very close Hanging Tower impending over the cloister.

In the Museum of the Cathedral are many works of art which were brought here from the Baptistery, the Cathedral and the Tower, so we manage to get the picture of the history of the above mentioned monumental buildings.

In the Museum we can see many Etruscan and Roman ruins, works coming from the East, beautiful *Illuminated Anthem Books,* wooden inlays, sculptures by Giovanni Pisano and by other artists who took part in the building of these monuments.

1. The house of the Canons

2. The Burgundian Crucifix

3. Tino di Camaiano: tomb-altar of San Ranieri

4. G. Pisano: Madonna with Child in ivory

5. the Hippogryph, a bronze sculpture of oriental origin

89

THE MONUMENTAL CEMETERY

The churchyard, which today is the seat of an important Museum, was started in 1278 on a project by Giovanni de Simone, more than anything to gather the Tombs of the noble Pisan families around the old Cemetery.

The Churchyard is divided from Piazza dei Miracoli by a long marble wall with blind arches; its pilaster strips are similar to the ones in the Baptistery, in the Cathedral and in the Tower. It is surmounted by a lovely Tabernacle by Giovanni Pisano representing *The Madonna and the Saints*.

On entering this building we are struck by the elegance of the arches overlooking the cemetery field, limiting the two huge galleries and their frescoed walls and containing statues and sarcophaguses of high artistic value. In the south side, in the *Salone degli Affreschi (i.e. Hall of the Frescoes),* we see the *Triumph of Death* and the *Last Judgement,* two lovely works by Buonamico Buffalmacco.

1. Aerial view of the Cemetery

2. The Tabernacle by Giovanni Pisano

1. Inside

1. Inside

2. A hall with frescos

3. A detail of the "Last Judgement": the Archangel Michael
separates the elected from the reprobates

4. A sarcophagus

THE MUSEUM OF THE SINOPITES

Sinopites are the first sketches of frescoes drawn on prepared walls. The name derives from the Turkish town of *Sinope* from which the reddish earths came from, which are used to make this particular colour, called in fact *Sinopia*.

The Museum is in a building looking on to the *Piazza dei Miracoli* built in 1257 on a project by Giovanni del Simone as a home for the sick and the poor. Later it was turned into a hospital. The museum develops on two floors in which it is possible to admire the sinopites made by Spinello Aretino, Benozzo Gozzoli, Taddeo Gaddi (a pupil of Giotto's) and most of all by Buonamico di Buffalmacco, whose fresco *The Last Judgement* is exposed next to its sinopite, therefore giving us a clear picture of the technique used for painting frescoes.

1. The entrance

2. Fresco

3. Stories of the Anchorets

4. The Last Judgement: six Apostles to the right of Jesus

PIAZZA DEI CAVALIERI

Piazza dei Cavalieri is a vast irregular square around which rise many artistically important buildings. The most imposing and important is the *Palazzo dei Cavalieri (i.e. Palace of the Knights)*, which today is the seat of the *Scuola Normale di Pisa*, built by Vasari in the 16th century. Opposite this palace are two works by Francavilla from the sameperiod: the *Fountain* and the *Statue of Cosimo I de' Medici* who had founded the *Ordine di Santo Stefano dei Cavalieri*

(i.e. Order of Saint Stephen of the Knights) in 1562. To the left is the nice *Palazzo dell'Orologio (i.e. Clock Palace)* and to the right is the *Chiesa di Santo Stefano dei Cavalieri (i.e. Church of Saint Stephen of the Knights)*, both built by Vasari.

1. Right: the Palace of the Knights opposite the Palace of the Clock
2. The Palace of the Knights seen from the front
3. A detail of the fountain and the statue to Cosimo I de' Medici

THE NATIONAL CHURCH OF SANTO STEFANO DEI CAVALIERI

Right of the *Palazzo dei Cavalieri (i.e. Palace of the Knights)* is the National Church of Santo Stefano dei Cavalieri designed by Vasari in the second half of the 16th century. The two side aisles were formerly devoted to changing-rooms for the *Knights of the Order of Saint Stephen.* Inside we can see trophies won by the Saracens and some *Figure-Heads* from the ships of the Knights' fleet. The lovely Pulpit by C. Fancelli is worth seeing.

National Church of Saint Stephen of the Knights: the façade

THE CHURCH OF SANTA MARIA DELLA SPINA

The Church of Santa Maria della Spina (spina means thorn) beares this name because for some time it contained a thorn from Jesus Crown on the Cross. It is a lovely example of Gothic art, placed on the Lungarno Gambacorti (the Lungarnos are the streets winding along the Arno river). It was built in 1323 by Lupo Capomaestro on the ruins of an ancient oratory.

Church of Santa Maria della Spina: façade

THE NATIONAL MUSEUM OF SAN MATTEO

The National Museum of San Matteo is placed on the banks of the Arno river, next to the beautiful *Palazzo Medici*. It is contained in a building which was originally a female Benedictine Monastery (notice its nice cloister).

It is one of the most important Museums in Italy for its collection of wooden sculptures, but it also contains beautiful marble sculptures and lovely paintings. Here we can see all the works of the Maestros from the 12th-13th century Pisan School such as Nicola, Giovanni, Andrea and Nino Pisano and Bonanno.

See the beautiful *Polyptich* by Simone Martini and a picture of *Saint Paul* by Masaccio painted on wood.

1. Museum-Church of San Matteo and Medici Palace

2. The hall of the statues in wood: "Announced Virgin" by Andrea Pisano, made in polychromatic wood

THE OLD CITTADELLA

After the destructions caused by the wars between Pisans and Florentines, the Old Cittadella was rebuilt by the latter towards the end of the 15th century. A century later Ferdinando I de' Medici changed it into an arsenal for the building of galleis for the fleet of the *Knights of Saint Stephen*.

THE LUMINARA AND THE HISTORIC REGATTA OF SAN RANIERI

The *luminara* takes place every year on the night between June 16th and 17th in honour of San Ranieri, the town's Patron Saint. It is a lovely event, during which all the buildings overlooking the Arno are lit up and the fireworks reflect their coloured lights in the water of the river.

On June 17th is the *Regata Storica (i.e. Historic Regatta)*, in which men dressed in historic costumes row richly decorated ancient boats.

1. Aerial view of the Cittadella (bottom left) and view of the town

2. Luminara and fires on the Arno river

3. Historic regatta of the Maritime Republics

VOLTERRA

The town of Volterra is placed on the highest ridge-line of the area, between the Valleys of the Cecina and of the Era rivers. It is one of the towns richest in Etruscan and Roman monuments.

Velathri (this is the name the Etruscans used for it) became the most powerful of the 12 *Lucumons* composing the *Etruscan Nation* for it extended its dominion to the south all the way down to Populonia and to the north right up to the mouths of the Magra river.

The Romans called it *Volterrae*.

The Etruscans fortified it, building 7 km long walls, of which we still see some sections, the most important of which is the *Porta dell'Arco (ie. Arch's Gate)*.

There are many traces dating back to the the Roman period, among which are the Theatre and the ruins of the Thermal Baths.

The *Cathedral* and the *Baptistery* (12th-13th century) in Piazza San Giovanni have reached us from the Middle Ages. Very particular is the Tower-House of the Buonparentis, and also the group of over-bridges connecting it to the other buildings, forming the so-called *Quadrivio dei Buonparenti*.

The real centre of town is the *Piazza dei*

1. Aerial view of the town: the imposing structure of the Medici Fortress in the foreground

2. Aerial view of the historic centre

3. Fiumi Park

Priori dominated by the homonymous Palace, which is Tuscany's most ancient *Palazzo Comunale (i.e. Town-Hall)*. It is typical for its lovely windows with two lights and for the majolica coats-of-arms of the Florentine Commissars, which are to be seen on the façade as well as on the imposing overhanging tower.

Opposite the *Palazzo dei Priori* rises the *Palazzo Pretorio (i.e. Praetorial Palace)* also surmounted by a crenellated tower.

The *Museo Guarnacci* is the most important museum in Italy for the presence of many ruins regarding the Etruscan, Villanovian and Roman Art and Civilization. The objects made of onix and alabaster, of which this area is rich, are all beautiful; the handcraft manufacture of these materials makes Volterra famous all around the world even in our time.

In the upper part of town we can see the imposing Fortress, characterized by the *Donjon* erected by Lorenzo the Magnificent next to the existing Rocca Vecchia (i.e. Old Fortress). Do not forget to

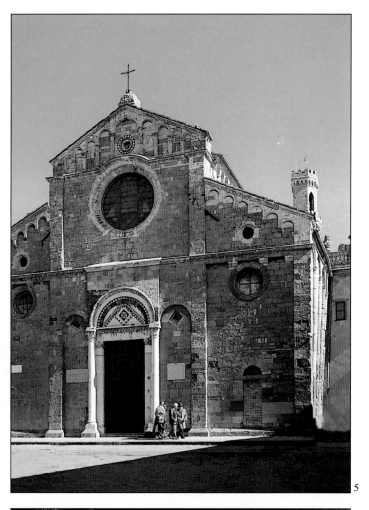

walk around the *Crags* dominated by the ancient *Bazia Camaldolese (i.e. Camaldolite Abbey)* which was abandoned for a long time; in fact, the chasm following the landslide which invested and buried entire Etruscan, Roman and Medieval towns came very close to its walls.

1. *The door of the Arch*
2. *Palazzo dei Priori*
3. *The Municipal Museum*
4. *The Roman Forum*
5. *The Cathedral*
6. *The Quadrivium by Buonparenti*
7. *The Guarnacci Museum: the Bride and Groom*
8. *Aerial view of the Balze and of the Camaldolite Abbey*

LIVORNO

Livorno is known all around the world for its famous Naval Academy, but maybe most of all for its training-ship *Amerigo Vespucci*, one of the most beautiful existing sailing-ships; it ploughs the seas of the entire world carrying a message of peace and fraternity; the crew is made up of young, perfectly trained cadet officers. The Academy was founded in 1881 by the General of the Naval Engineers, Benedetto Brin.

The town has a mainly modern aspect for it was almost completely rebuilt after the destruction caused by the aerial and naval bombing during World War II. But in the old part of town there are still many monuments from the past, specially from the times of the Medici family who provided Livorno with a definitive urban aspect in the 16th century; they reactivated the port and made it efficient, so much so that still

today it is the lung of the local economy.
The first historical outline on the *Livorna* village, a fraction of the Pisan Port, dates back to 904 AD. In the 14th century the Pisans turned it into a fortified port and the Medicis, who gave it a definitive aspect, bought it from the Genoese in 1421.
In 1577 Francesco I de' Medici started to rebuild the Medici town around the ancient Pisan Castle, surrounded by the *Moats*.

1. Aerial view of the town

2. The Monument to the "Four Moors"

In spite of the destructions due to the war, the town has kept its urban system intact, whereas unfortunately many monuments were destroyed. The two fortresses, some Churches and some Palaces, as well as the monument to Ferdinando I (better known as I *Quattro Mori (i.e. The Four Moors)* were saved.

As we said before, the Medicis made the old port very efficient, and therefore it has become the most important Tuscan port for maritime trade. Thanks to the customs facilities that were established, the port became the favourite destination of many foreign tradesmen.

By the end of the 18th century Livorno became the second most important and populated town in Tuscany, after Florence. After the annexion to the Kingdom of Italy, at the end of the last century, industrial and tourist activities started to thrive and were further encouraged after World War II, so now Livorno is a very important harbour centre, as well as the outlet for metallurgical and oil plants in this area.

Even the local navy-yards are famous.

1. The Old Fortress

2. The Town Hall

3. The Cathedral

1

Do not miss to see the *Cathedral,* the *Piazza Grande* and the *Palazzo Comunale (i.e. Town-Hall)* built in 1720 on a project by Giovanni del Fantasia, characterized by an imposing marble double staircase. See the lovely *Palazzo Mascagni,* today the seat of the *Acquario Comunale (i.e. Municipal Acquarium)* and the homonymous terrace over the sea devoted to the great Maestro.

In Piazza Micheli we can see the lovely statue devoted to the Grand Duke Ferdinando I created by Giovanni Bondini (1595). In 1626 the very famous *Four Moors* engraved by Pietro Tacca were added at the foot of the monument.

To visit the Old and the New Fortress, both built by the Medicis respectively in 1521 and 1590, it is necessary to walk along the famous *Moats,* the most famous of which is the *Fosso Reale (ie. Royal Moat),* built in the same period for a better defence of the fortresses. See the lovely *Sanctuary of Montenero,* placed on the homonymous hill from which we see a fantastic view.

2

3

1. *Aerial view of the tourist port*

2. *Piazza Grande seen from the sea*

3. *Sea-storm on the Mascagni terrace*

4. *One of the "Fossi" (i.e. Moats)*

5. *A detail of the "Four Moors"*

6. *The Amerigo Vespucci at anchor*

7. *The Amerigo Vespucci at sea*

8. *The "Calafuria" tower*

9. *The Montenero Sanctuary*

Pictures 2-3-4-5-6-8-9 by V.Bellucci
Picture nr 7 by Comm. Giambruni

4

7

5

8

6

9

ISOLA D' ELBA

The Isola d'Elba (i.e. Isle of Elba) is the largest and most important island of the Tuscan Archipelago, as well as the third largest Italian island. It is separated from the continent by the 10 km wide Piombino Canal. It is therefore easily reachable from Piombino itself, after about a one hour pleasant crossing by ferry. For a few years now, it has been possible to reach the Island by airplane, but only from some Italian towns.

Elba is 27 km long (from Punta Nera to Capo Ortona) and 18 km wide (from Capo della Vita to Punta dei Ripalti). It is characterized by never-ending hills and mountains, the highest of which is Monte Capanne (1019 m); it is full of springs which nourish a very vigorous Mediterranean flora.

In the subsoil there are many minerals, therefore first the Etruscans and then the Romans started to exploit the mines.

The Isle of Elba is also renowned because Napoleon Bonaparte was exiled here from May 3rd 1814 to February 26th 1815; he lived near Portoferraio, first in the *Villa dei Mulini* and then in *Villa San Martino*.

Thanks to its beaches, its clean sea and its mild and never sultry climate, the Isola d'Elba is now the favourite destination of may tourists who invade the local villages after having enjoyed the sun on the sandy beaches and explored the lovely sounding-depths.

PORTOFERRAIO

Portoferraio is the chief town and main port of the Island. It is placed on a lovely and vast glade and dominated by the Falcone and Stella Fortresses built by Cosimo I de' Medici to defend the town from the pirates.

Being a natural port, it was used first by the Greeks, then by the Etruscans and later by the Romans to embark the metal and granite which the Island is rich of.

PORTO AZZURRO

Thanks to its position opposite Piombino and to the fact of being placed on a charming natural bay protected from the wind, Porto Azzurro has become the second most important port of the Island since World War II and it is visited mainly by passenger ferries. The town is dominated by the Fortress of San Giacomo, also known as Longone, built in the shape of a star by Philip III of Spain in 1603. Until 1947 in fact its name was Porto Longone, but the inhabitants demanded it to be changed into Porto Azzurro.

4

MARCIANA MARINA

Marciana Marina is a typical fisherman's town with a small port dominated by a Tower built by the Pisans in the 12th century. Today Marciana Marina is one of the island's most popular seaside resorts. See the typical *Quartiere del Cotone (i.e. Cotton District)*.

5

1. *Portoferraio*

2. *The gulf of Procchio*

3. *La Biodola Gulf*

4. *Marciana Marina*

5. *Porto Azzurro*

6. *Cavo*

6

CASTIGLIONCELLO

Castiglioncello is a delightful seaside resort, a few km south of Livorno.
Sandy beaches scattered with vegetation and beautiful cliffs wind uninterruptedly along the coast. Castiglioncello, Marina di Campolacciano, Portovecchio and Coletta form a very attractive tourist resort.

Aerial view of Castiglioncello and of the coast all the way to Livorno

MARINA DI CECINA

Marina di Cecina is part of the Municipality of Cecina, placed further upstream along the two sides of the Via Aurelia. It is one of the most important seaside resorts of the *Riviera degli Etruschi,* placed at the mouth of the homonymous river and provided with a fully-equipped tourist port.
In the courtyard of the Palazzo Comunale (i.e. Town-Hall) we can see a perfect reconstruction of the *Tomba di Casaglia (i.e. Casaglia Tomb),* found in the surroundings and dating back to the 6th century bC.
Other Etruscan-Roman ruins can be seen in the *Villa delle Cinquantina,* an ancient Grand Ducal farm placed in the neighbouring village of San Pietro in Palazzi. The ruins of an important Roman building certainly used as thermal baths (as proved by the *Tepidarium* and an underground *Tank*) have recently been found in the village of San Vincenzino.

Aerial view of the canal port, the tourist port and the town

BOLGHERI

The peaceful village of Bolgheri can be reached from the Via Aurelia after having driven for about five km down an alley at the sides of which grow grand cypress trees, quoted by the poet Giosuè Carducci in his Ode *Davanti a San Guido (i.e. In front of San Guido)*. The town is dominated by the grand Castle of the Della Gherardesca family, who were the Lords from the 11th century. See the nice house in which Giosuè Carducci lived between 1838 and 1848. Opposite the alley leading to Bolgheri rises the *Chapel of San Guido* built in 1703 on an octagonal plan. It strikes the by-passers because it stands out elegant and isolated among the secular trees.

CASTAGNETO CARDUCCI DONORATICO

Even the town of Castagneto Carducci rising in the hilly inland owes its fame to Giosuè Carducci who lived here for a year. To remember him, in 1907 the Municipality had the poet's name added onto the original name Castagneto.

In Castagneto too is a castle which used to belong to the Della Gherardesca family. The centre of town is still typically Medieval; we come to it through an *Arch* surmounted by a tabernacle. Do not forget to visit the lovely *Parrocchiale di San Lorenzo (i.e. Parish Church of San Lorenzo)* and the *Oratorio del Crocifisso (i.e. Oratory of the Crucifix)*.

Along the coast rises the delightful town of Donoratico-Marina di Castagneto, which is renowned for its lovely beach and for the *Gulliver Park* with its *Cavallino Matto* fun-fair where the children and grown-up go after a day at the sea.

See the interesting ruins of the 10th century *Donoratico Castle* which is famous because Count Ugolino Della Gherardesca was kept here after having been defeated by the Pisans in the Meloria naval battle (1284).

1. the row of cypress trees leading from the Aurelia to Bolgheri

2. Bolgheri

3. Castagneto Carducci

MASSA MARITTIMA

Placed along the street leading from the Maremma to Siena, at the foot of the most southern part of the Metalliferous Hills, Massa Marittima is divided into two parts: *Massa Vecchia (i.e. Old Massa)* and *Massa Nuova (i.e. New Massa)* which is higher up in the hills. In this area there are many Etruscan and Roman ruins, for already then did these populations exploit the many surrounding mines. In Massa Vecchia rise the beautiful *Palazzo Comunale (i.e. Town-Hall)* and the *Casa dei Conti di Biserno (i.e. House of the Counts of Biserno),* connected to each other by a tower: the two buildings date back to the 13th century. Also notice the *Palazzo Pretorio (i.e. Praetorial Palace)* from the same period; it has now become the seat of a *Museo Archeologico (i.e. Archaeological Museum).* The beautiful *Cathedral of San Cerbone* contains paintings attributed to the school of Duccio di Boninsegna, or maybe even to the Maestro himself. In Massa Nuova, which is connected to the Old part by means of a 14th century "Porta di Silici", see the interesting "Church of Sant'Agostino" and the "Palazzo delle Armi (i.e. Palace of the Weapons)" containing a museum devoted to the minerary activity, where hundreds of rock and mineral samples have been collected.

1. The Cathedral

2. The Town-Hall

CAMPIGLIA MARITTIMA

Even the lovely town of Campiglia Marittima is rich in Etruscan, Roman and Medieval history. It is placed in an elevated position and it is characterized by the flights of stairs connecting the various floors of the village built along the mountain slope, as well as by the narrow alleys which constitute the urban system. The *Palazzo Pretorio (i.e. Praetorial Palace)* contains a *Mineral Exhibition*, for this area is full of minerals and stones.

Worthy of notice is also the Romanesque style *Pieve di San Giovanni (i.e. Parish of San Giovanni)* built in the 12th century.

1. Parish church of San Giovanni

2. Praetorial Palace

THE ARCHAEOLOGICAL MINE PARK OF SAN SILVESTRO

Leaving from Campiglia Marittima or from San Vincenzo we reach the Park of San Silvestro which is being restored to protect this extraordinary open air museum.

Thanks to the excavations of the ancient village and of the nearby mines, a miner and smelter's village from the Middle Ages was discovered. Visiting the village and the mines which were exploited ever since the Etruscan times, we realize what the life of a poor community must have been like in these impervious areas, extracting, smelting and processing metal.

The Park is managed by the *Val di Cornia SpA,* created thanks to the collaboration of local bodies, the University of Siena, the Province, the State, the European Community and private citizens.

1 The park offices

2. The San Silvestro fortress

3. The entrance to the "Temperino" mine

We would like to thank the Val di Cornia SpA who helped us with the text and pictures nr 2 and 3

POPULONIA - BARATTI

Populonia-Baratti is one of the most important and better preserved Etruscan settlements in this area. It started as a colony of Volterra placed in a rised position over the lovely Gulf of Baratti. From Populonia we can enjoy a lovely view of the Cornia Valley, of the Baratti Gulf, of the strong buttresses in the Metalliferous Hills and of the Isle of Elba.

The Etruscan town developed on two different levels: on the highest was the *Acropoli (i.e. Acropolis)* surrounded by walls; by the sea a well-equipped port was built. In the 3rd century bC Populonia-Baratti fell under the domination of the Romans (there are many traces of their presence, too) and in the following centuries it underwent a relentless decline because it was sacked and destroyed especially by the Longobards who then razed it to ther ground.

The first discovery of the ancient *Necropoli (i.e. Necropolis)* occurred at the beginning of this century, when many tombs were found near the *Poggio della Porcareccia* and in the farm of the *San Cerbone,* as well as in the *Malassina* and *Granate* hillocks. Among these tombs we recall the *Tomba dei Carri (i.e. Tomb of the Carts),* so called because some war carts were found inside it; the tomb of the *Letti Funebri (i.e. Funeral Beds)* and of the *Bronzetto di Offerenti* in the shape of a shrine. Another very important one is the *Tomba dei Flabelli,* so called because some bronze-plated fans were found inside it. From the Middle Ages, beyond the town's urban structure, we still have the ancient *Fortress* placed in a dominant and panoramic position, characterized by strong walls and by an imposing crenellated tower.

Nowadays, thanks to its lovely sandy shore surrounded by an abundant pine-forest and thanks to its deep waters, the Gulf of Baratti has become one of the favourite destinations of bathers, deep-sea divers and tourists who anchor their boats in this lovely natural port and enjoy the view of the ancient ruins and pretty hills all around.

1. The town and the fortress seen from the airplane

2. The archaeological sight

3. The "Bronzetto di Offerenti" tomb

4. The lovely gulf of Baratti

PIOMBINO

Placed on the most southern part of the homonymous promontory, Piombino closes the wide Gulf of Follonica to the north. Piombino is the closest and most important shipment port to the Isle of Elba. In Roman times Piombino was called *Porto Falesia*. Its typically Medieval historic centre and all the monuments from that time are very interesting. Among the latter we mention the *Porta di Sant'Antonio (i.e. Gate of Sant'Antonio)* which is an integral part of a Tower from 1213, and the 13th century *Palazzo Comunale (i.e. Town Hall)* flanked by the lovely *Torre dell'Orologio (i.e. Clock Tower)* built in 1598. To the east of the town rises the *Castle* erected by the Borgias at the beginning of the 16th century. Near the Castle we find *Piazzale Bovio*, a lovely natural terrace stretching into the sea. Very interesting are also the ruins of the ancient *Chiesa dell'Annunziata (i.e. Church of the Virgin Mary)* contained in the building of the old hospital which is now abandoned. Near the Small Port rises the lovely *Fontana dei Canali (i.e. Fountain of the Canals)* which was built by the Pisans in 1247. Opposite a marble fountain built in 1468, in the nearby *Piazza Cittadella* is a beautiful Renaissance *Chapel* decorated with lovely sculptures; it was built on a quadrangular plan and has coats-of-arms and bas-relief figures of the *Appiani* family, the former Lords of the Town. In our days, Piombino is even an important seaside resort and it is provided with many beaches, the most famous of which is Salivoli.

1. The small port and Piazza Bovio seen from the stronghold
2. The Rivellino

FOLLONICA

The ample Gulf extending between the Promontory of Piombino to the north and Punta Ala to the south owes its name to the town of Follonica.

In Medieval times, as of the 15th century, Follonica belonged to the *Appiani* family who around the 16th century built a mill and an iron-foundry in which the minerals from the Isola d'Elba were processed.

Do not forget to see the 19th century *Parish church of San Leopoldo* preceded by an important *Pronaos* partly made of cast iron. And also the *Municipal Library* which contains some wooden models of industrial plants from the 19th century.

Today Follonica is a very famous seaside resort, thanks to the beautiful sea and the vast pine-forests surrounding it.

1. The seaside
2. Aerial view

VETULONIA

Vetulonia, one of the most important towns of Maritime Etruria, was formerly known as *Vatluna* or *Vetluna*. It is believed that the symbols of power, the lictor's fasces and the curule chair were born here and then assimilated by the Romans.

Of the old Etruscan *Acropolis* we can still see the *Mura dell'Arce (i.e. Citadel Walls)* composed of enormous polygonal blocks.

In the vast necropolis we find *winze* as well as *tumulus* tombs which are most probably from the 7th century bC.

Until now five cemeteries have been discovered: in Poggio alla Guardia, in Poggio alle Biebe, in Poggio al Bello, in Colle Baroncio and in Costa delle Dupiane.

About 3 km from Vetulonia are another two imposing tombs: the *Tumulo della Pietrera* and the *Tumulo del Diavolino,* which were both discovered by the archaeologist Falchi towards the end of the 19th century.

From the Middle Ages to 1887 Vetulonia was called Colonna, then it regained its ancient name because of the archaeological discoveries started by Isidoro Falchi in 1884. In Vetulonia we also see much evidence of the Medieval period during which the *Parish Church* and its annexed *Bell-Tower* were built.

1. The Parish Church

2. Excavations in Poggiarello-Renzetti

3. The Pietrera Grave

4. Tomb of Diavolino II

112

PUNTA ALA

Punta Ala is very much decentralized compared to the main roads, therefore it has mantained a very natural aspect, also because the town-planners who created it were very clever in integrating the residential part in the lovely natural element.

Provided with a very well equipped Tourist Port, it is a permanent and occasional seat for many tourists who can go from Punta Ala to all the nearby islands of the Tuscan Archipelago, as well as to all the numerous bays along the neighbouring coast-line.

Equipped also with lovely collective sport areas for golf, riding, polo and other sports, Punta Ala has become the *reserve* of an exclusive public.

1-2. Aerial views of the tourist port and its surroundings

CASTIGLIONE DELLA PESCAIA

Castiglione della Pescaia is characterized by a vast Canal Port which some scholars state was the ancient Etruscan settlement of *Hasta* and then, in Roman times, *Portus Traianus*.

The town extends along the two sides of the canal port; it is composed of a modern part extending to the thick pine-forest of Tombolo to the right, whereas to the left it climbs up the *Poggio Petricco* and becomes a Medieval town called *Castiglione Castello;* this higher part of town is surrounded by strong walls and dominated by the grand *Rocca Aragonese (i.e. Aragonese Fortress)* (14th-15th century) whose enormous corner towers stretch perpendicularly over the sea.

Castiglione della Pescaia was handed over to the *Abbey of Sant'Antimo* by Ludovico il Pio in the 9th century; then it passed under the rule of the Pisans who built a fortress and governed here until the beginning of the 15th century, when it passed under the domination of the Florentine Republic on request of its citizens.

In 1447 the town was occupied by the Aragonese who then gave it to Pope Pius II.

It was dominated first by the Senese and later by the Florentines; it was then annexed to the Grand Duchy of Tuscany. The Grand Duke Leopoldo II started the works of drainage of the ancient *Lacus Prilius* which had become marshland in the course of the centuries.

1. The Castle
2. Aerial view

114

ROSELLE

The traces of the very ancient Etruscan-Roman town of Roselle are to be found a few km from Grosseto, on the *Poggio di Moscona*. Roselle was part of the Etruscan *Dodecapoli*. All around this area even the ruins of the ancient town of Villanovia di Nomadelfia are to be found. Remembered by famous historians such as Aligi of Alicarnasso and Tito Livio, Roselle became a Roman colony in 294 bC, then a federate town until the *Lex Julia*. In the 5th century AD it became an episcopal seat, but in the 12th century it was destroyed by the Saracens and the Longobards.

As soon as we enter the archaeological area, we are struck by the enormous *City Walls* which were built with huge irregular blocks of limestone for a length of over 3,000 metres. The first building is believed to date back to the 6th century bC, but the marks of later times are evident too. There are traces of six doors and of patrol trenches in the highest point, at a hight of seven metres.

At the centre of the depression between two hills we find the well-kept ruins of the *Foro Romano (i.e. Roman Forum),* of a *Basilica,* of a small *Anfitheatre,* of the *Thermal Baths* and of the *Augusteum.*

1. The Anfitheatre
2. View of the excavations
3. Aerial view of the Archaeological sight

115

GROSSETO

Grosseto is placed in the lower part of the plain of the Ombrone river and it has always been considered the real chief-town of the Maremma. In the early Middle Ages Grosseto was a small fortified village built along the Maremma road leading from Rome to Pisa. It underwent an enormous expansion after the Saracins destroyed the ancient town of Roselle in 935. The citizens of Roselle sought refuge in Grosseto and so Innocent II transferred the Episcopal seat there. From the 9th century it belonged to the *Aldobrandeschi* family.

In 1336 it was conquered by the Senese who expelled *Vanni degli Abati's* family from town. After the bloody battle of Montalcino, Grosseto, which was the last stronghold to give up its weapons to the Florentines, passed under the power of the Medicis in 1559. With this great Florentine family Grosseto knew a period of economic and demographic revival, especially with Francesco I who started the first works of drainage and reclamation of the surrounding marshlands.

The city centre is surrounded by stronG walls in the shape of a hexagon built by the Grand Duke of Tuscany Francesco I on a project by the architect Baldassare Lanci in 1574. The walls are reinforced by 6 ramparts, of which the north-east one contains the *Fortezza Medicea (i.e. Medici Fortress)*. In the 13th-14th century *Church of San Francesco* we can see a crucifix by Duccio da Boninsegna. See the nearby *Cloister* dominated by the slim Bell-Tower.

The *Museo Archeologico della Maremma (i.e. Maremma Archaeological Museum)*, surely the most important museum in

1. The Medici Fortress

2. Palace of the Province and monument to Dante

3. Aerial view. Notice the strong Medici walls surrounding the historic centre

this area, contains Etruscan and Roman ruins gathered in all the surrounding settlements. In the section dedicated to Medieval history we can see paintings and sculptures from the Florentine, Pisan and Senese schools. In spite of the many restorations it has undergone, the *Cathedral of San Lorenzo,* built in 1190 by the architect Sozzo Pace Rustichino, is still a remarkable example of Romanesque-Gothic architectonic beauty. See the lovely *Palazzo Comunale (i.e. Town-Hall)* built in 1870 and the Monument to Leopold II erected in honour of the Grand Duke (he tried to wipe out malaria and drain the Maremma).

1. The Cathedral
2. The Archaeological Museum: an Etruscan sarcophagus
3. Church of San Francesco

THE NATURAL PARK OF THE MAREMMA

The Natural Park of the Maremma is one of the most beautiful naturalistic oases in Italy and it extends for about 10,000 hectars between the sea and the Via Aurelia, between the mouth of the Ombrone river and the Talamone Promontory. It is full of vast pine-forests and damp areas and it is dominated by the *Monti dell'Uccellina* which often fall sheer to the sea. The park is closed and can be visited only if accompanied by the guides of the *Centro Visite di Albarese;* Albarese is known because every year on May 1st it hosts the *Merca del bestiame brado (i.e. Wild Cattle Market)* during which the *Butteri (i.e. local cowherds)* break and brand the wild horses and bulls in a show very much enjoyed by the tourists.

Visiting the park we are enchanted by the incontaminate nature as well as by the many traces witnessing how in ancient times even this area was inhabited by man. Important elements from the bronze age have been found in the *Grotta dello Scoglietto* which reminds us of the presence of man in different times in history.

See the lovely *Torre Marsilia (i.e. Marsilia Tower)* on the hill of Collecchio which recalls the story of Margherita Marsili: she was kidnapped in 1543 by the Saracen pirate Khair An-Din called Barbarossa, taken to Costantinople and locked up in the harem of the Sultan Soliman II the Magnificent because he wanted her to become his favourite and then wife. Their son Selim II became the Emperor of the Ottoman Empire and took part in the famous naval battle of Lepanto in 1571.

The grandest ruins, though, are those of the 12th century *Abbazia Benedettina di San Rabano (i.e. Benedictine Abbey of San Rabano),* of the *Torre dell'Uccellina* and of the ancient *Monastery of San Galgano* who were destroyed by the Senese in 1438. This imposing group of ruins is placed at the top of the Uccellina Mount.

1. Mount Uccellina: on its peak are the ruins of the Marsilia Tower and of the Abbey of San Rabano

2-3. Scenes from the wild cattle market in Alborese

4. San Rabano

TALAMONE

Called *Tlamu* by the Etruscans and *Telamon* by the Romans, the ancient town of Talamone rose on the hill of Talamonaccio on the eastern side of the bay. In 82 bC it was destroyed by Silla who wanted to revenge himself for the hospitality offered to Mario during his escape from Africa. It was rebuilt only in Medieval times in its present position, on a rocky promontory opposite the Argentario, thus forming a lovely Gulf in which the river Aldegna flows. It was at first dominated by the *Priorato dell'Abbazia di San Salvatore (i.e. Priorate of the Abbey of San Salvatore),* then by the Aldobrandeschi family, by the Senese, the Genoese and finally by the Grand Dukes of Tuscany.

In 1860 Garibaldi stopped in Talamone during the crossing which took him to Sicily, to fill up his ships with weapons and food.

The modern town of Talamone is equipped with a port for fishing boats and a tourist port, and it is still dominated by the *Castle* (which falls sheer to the sea) and by the strong walls surrounding the entire town. The castle and the walls were built by the Senese between the 14th and the 15th century on a project by famous architects, among which we name Vecchietta.

1-3. Two lovely aerial views

2. The Castle

MAGLIANO IN TOSCANA

Magliano in Toscana is another of the many towns in the Maremma which has been enriched by history. The Etruscans called it *Hepa* whereas the Romans called it *Heba*; in the Middle Ages it was built to look as we see it today.

Magliano in Toscana was ruled by the *Aldobrandeschi* family who ordered the still existing walls, which were then remanaged by *Bibbiena* in the 15th century. Inside the walls rises the historic centre with all its palaces, among which we recall the *Palazzo dei Priori* remembered for its *Maglio (i.e. Mallet)*, the town's symbol, hanging over the ogival portal. Remember the *Church of San Giovanni Battista*, the one of the *Annunziata (i.e. Virgin Mary)* and the one of *San Martino* rising near the homonymous hill. They are all of Romanesque origin (11th century) and have been restored later in the course of the centuries, therefore they also have some Gothic and Renaissance aspects.

Immediately outside the walls are the grand ruins of the *Church of San Bruzio*, which was started in the 11th century but never completed.

Etruscan and Roman findings were discovered in the nearby *Necropolis of Marsiliana*. Finely decorated gold and ivory objects were found in beautiful tombs dating back to the 8th and 7th century bC. The most important element from the Roman period is a 1st century bronze board called *Tabula Hebana*.

1. Magliano: the Church of San Giovanni

2. Saturnia: the thermal springs

3. Saturnia: the park and the swimmingpool

4. Saturnia: the Aldobrandeschi family castle

SATURNIA

In spite of its very ancient origins, Saturnia owes its present fame to the *Thermal Baths* which were used already by the Romans.

Placed in the inland, in the heart of the Maremma, it is surrounded by green and abundant hills. Called *Aurinia* by the Etruscans, Saturnia was an annexe of Vulci. Conquered by the Romans in 280 bC, it became a dominion of the Longobards, the Aldobrandeschis and finally the Senese.

There are still today some tracts of the ancient walls. Do visit *Villa Ciacci* near the Cassero (i.e. Quarter-deck) for it contains an interesting collection of Etruscan and Roman ruins. Even the *Parish Church* of Romanesque origin is beautiful.

SOVANA

This town of Etruscan origin had its maximum splendour in the 7th and 6th century bC; in the 3rd century bC it was conquered by the Romans.

The present aspect of Sovana is that of a lovely Medieval village. The heart of the historic centre is the *Piazza Pretoria* on which rise next to one another the *Palazzo Pretorio (i.e. Praetorial Palace)* with its façade covered with coats-of-arms, the *Loggetta del Capitano (i.e. Captain's Small Loggia)* decorated by a large coat-of-arms with the symbols of the Medicis, the *Palazzo dell'Archivio (i.e. Archive Palace)* characterized by a small Bell-Tower, and finally the small but delightful *Church of Santa Maria*. All these buildings date back to the 12th and 13th century. Immediately outside the ancient walls we find the 14th century *Rocca Aldobrandesca (i.e. Fortress of the Aldobrandis)* and the *Duomo dei S.S. Pietro e Paolo (i.e. Cathedral of Saint Peter and Saint Paul)* from the same time, rebuilt on an existing 9th century building.

Fragments of ancient walls as well as a nearby Necropolis in which we can see many Chapel Tombs, have reached us from Etruscan and Roman times. The most important tombs are the *Ildebranda,* the *Tifone* and the *Sirena,* all dating back to the 3rd and 2nd century bC.

1. The fortress of the Aldobrandeschi family

2. The Cathedral

PITIGLIANO

Built on a high ridge-line between the valleys of the rivers Lante and Melata, Pitigliano may seem to the tourist's eye like one of the many typically Medieval villages, perhaps vaguely similar to San Giminiano. In fact, even in Pitigliano there are many Tower-Houses standing out evocatively against the sky.

There are only a few ruins from the Etruscan-Roman period, such as some parts of the old walls near the *Porta Capo di Sotto.* In the nearby areas, though, there are more important traces.

In the Middle Ages it was part of the Aldobrandeschi feud. The main trace in town was left by the Orsini family, who elected Pitigliano to County Capital. Pitigliano has been the theatre of many battles between the Orsinis and the Colonnas and the Borgias.

The imposing *Palazzo Orsini* is connected to the *Citadella* by means of the arches of an ancient acqueduct. See the lovely *Duomo dei S.S. Pietro e Paolo (i.e. Cathedral of Saint Peter and Saint Paul)* and the *Church of Santa Maria.*

1. View

2. The Orsini family fortress

ORBETELLO

Orbetello overlooks a lovely lagoon, a real natural oasis in which many rare birds find their natural habitat. The lagoon is composed of the *Giannella Tombolo (to the north) and Feniglia Tombolo (to the south):* these two earth platforms connect the dry-land to the Monte Argentario. Orbetello too is connected to the Argentario by means of an artificial rural dam, which is about 1,500 m long and was built in 1842.

Orbetello's origins are very old; the polygonal walls of the eastern promenade and some ruins of an ancient village from the 6th century bC lead us to believe that there existed a blooming Etruscan centre.

In Roman times it belonged to the 7th Regione Augustea (i.e. Augustan Region).

In the early Middle Ages it first belonged to the Byzantines and then to the Longobards. After that it passed under the rule of the Aldobrandeschis, then of the Orsinis, the Senese, and finally it was conquered by the Spaniards in 1555. Between 1557 and 1620, during the reigns of Philip II and Philip III, the Spaniards built some imposing defence fortresses here: their walls with the lovely *Porta del Soccorso* and the powder-magazine placed on the wet-dock can still be seen; this is exactly the place from which 25 *Savoia Marchetti* sea planes took off guided by Italo Balbo, and then arrived in Chicago between July 1st and August 12th 1933.

From 1736 Orbetello was part of the Reign of the Borbonis and as of 1815 it became part of the Grand Duchy of Tuscany.

Do not forget to visit the *Civico Antiquarium* in which Etruscan and Roman ruins are gathered, and the beautiful *Cathedral* erected in 1376 on the base of an ancient Christian Temple. The Cathedral was rebuilt in the 17th century when two side aisles and the imposing *Torre dell'Orologio (i.e. Clock Tower)* were added on.

1. Aerial view of the Argentario

2. Aerial view: top left the dam outside the harbour connecting Orbetello to the Argentario

3. The Cathedral Portal

4. The Etruscan walls

PORTO S. STEFANO

In 1842 Leopoldo II of Lorena elected Porto Santo Stefano to Municipality for the whole Argentario.

Porto Santo Stefano is placed on the south side of the Argentario and is connected to the mainland by means of the *Tombolo di Giannella* stretching out to the village of *Santa Liberata;* nearby are the ruins of an ancient *Roman Villa* of the *Domizi Enobarbs* who reigned here in the 1st century bC.

The historic centre is dominated by the imposing *Rocca Aragonese (i.e. Aragonese Fortress)* and surrounded by the strong walls built by the Spaniards in the 16th century as part of the defence system of the entire Monte Argentario.

1-2-3. Views of Porto Santo Stefano and its surroundings

COASTS OF THE ARGENTARIO

From Porto Santo Stefano towards Porto Ercole we cover a winding coastal road, which falls sheer to the sea and offers fantastic views. About half way we meet the *Forte Stella* built by the Spaniards as one of the defence strong points of the *State of the Garrisons.* It has recently been restored and in future it will be turned into a Museum with the most modern sound and video equipment to illustrate the history of the Argentario. Take a look at the *Faraglione della Maddalena,* the *Scoglio dell'Argentarolo* and the *Isola Rossa (i.e. Red Island)* so called for the reddish reflections of its rocks.

The view is interrupted by ancient sighting Towers, for the Argentario Mountain, which reaches into the sea, was considered a real *Sentry over the Mediterranean.*

1. Part of the western coast with tourist villages

2. A defence tower along the coast

3. The Cala di Gesso tower and, in the background, the Argentario rock

4. The red island at dawn

124

PORTO ERCOLE

Porto Ercole is the second most important town on the Argentario. It is placed on the eastern side of the Mountain and is connected to the mainland by means of the lovely *Tombolo della Feniglia* on which we find a magnificent sandy shore and a very thick pine-forest.

Porto Ercole overlooks a beautiful gulf enclosed between two promontories: one is surmounted by the strong Fortress and by the ancient Village, whereas the other, which divides it from the *Marina di Cala Galera,* is dominated by the *Forte Filippo II (i.e. Philip II Fortress).* The two fortresses were built by the Spaniards in the 16th century together with the neighbouring *Forte Stella* and *Forte Santa Barbara.*

The ancient village which has kept its Medieval aspect, reaches from the *Molo di Santa Barbara* to the *Rocca.* In the highest point of town rises the beautiful *Chiesa Parrocchiale di Sant'Erasmo* in which Michelangelo Merisi called *Il Caravaggio* was buried when he died of malaria at the age of 37 on the nearby Feniglia beach.

1-4. Aerial views

2-3. Typical streets in town

MARINA
DI CALA GALERA

The very well-equipped *Marina di Cala Galera* has been built near Porto Ercole; it is a well-protected natural bay and it seems to have been the outlet onto the sea for the neighboring Vetulonia. Also thanks to the two large artificial piers, the Marina is a secure refuge for over 700 boats of every size. It was inaugurated in 1975 and now it has become the seat of the *Circolo Nautico* which organizes many world-known regattas.

1. *Cala Galera: the promontory with the Fortress of Philip II's and Porto Ercole*

2. *The Marina of Cala Galera*

ISOLA DI GIANNUTRI

Even the small Island of Giannutri was lived on by the Greeks who called it *Artemisia* and by the Romans who called it *Dianium*. We can still see the ruins of an ancient Roman port near the *Cala dello Spalmatoio*, the main landing-place on the north-east part of the Island. Vestiges of an ancient Roman wet-dock are to be seen even near the *Cala Maestra*, in the north-west side of the Island. This area made of steep coasts is dominated by the ruins of a grand *Imperial Villa* placed at the centre of the *Archaeological Park of Giannutri*.
Giannutri was deserted for a long time, but now it has become the seat of a holiday-village and of many private villas.

1. A bay

2. Cala Maestra with the rests of the Roman wet dock

3. The archaeological park with the rests of the Imperial Villa

4. The grottos

127

ISOLA DEL GIGLIO

Many elements lead us to believe that the Isola del Giglio, which is the second largest isle in the Tuscan Archipelago, has been lived on ever since the Etruscan and Roman Enobarbs ruled in the Argentario.

It has a very rich Mediterranean vegetation and its temperate climate (never below freezing in winter and hardly ever above 25 centigrades in summer) make it the favourite destination of many tourists who circumnavigate this island to visit its numerous bays and creeks; its sounding-depths are full of fish, therefore it is a Paradise for fishermen and for submarine photographers. A residential tourism is developing mainly around the charming port dominated by the imposing *Torre del Lazzaretto,* as well as in the vast sandy shore of *Baia Campese.* On a small island near the shore rises the *Torre del Campese* erected by Ferdinando I of Borbone as defence from the Tunisian barbarian pirates.

1. Giglio Port

2. The ancient Medieval village surrounded by walls from the same period

3. Baia Campese: in the foreground rises the Torre del Campese

4. A detail of the granitic coasts

COSA - ANSEDONIA

The Roman town of *Cosa*, founded in 273 bC, was discovered in 1948 thanks to the escavations and the research carried out by the *American Academy* of Rome. Placed on the hill of Ansedonia, Cosa still presents strong walls in which we recognize the *Porta Romana (i.e. Roman Gate)*. Inside we find the *Forum* with some traces of the *Curia*, of the *Tempio della Concordia (i.e. Temple of Concord)* and of an ancient *Basilica*. In the *Acropolis* which is placed higher up, we find the ruins of the *Capitolium* and of a market.

Descending towards the sea, we can see the *Tagliata Etrusca:* a work of high hydraulic engineering composed of a trench dug into the rock to protect the downflow at sea of the *Burano Lake* emissary and prevent the silting up of the port. The river stretches to the sea through the *Spacco della Regina,* a deep natural cleft modified by the Romans.

Not far away rises the *Torre della Tagliata (i.e. Tower of the Tagliata)* which is famous because Giacomo Puccini used to stay here during his hunting sessions in the Maremma.

The modern Ansedonia was created holding in mind the way it was lived in by the Romans who had built many villas in the green hills. The most famous of these is the *Villa delle Sette Finestre (i.e. Villa of the Seven Windows),* so called for the seven arched porch openings onto the garden.

This is an exclusively residential complex from which we enjoy a fantastic view.

See the *Torre di San Pancrazio (i.e. Tower of San Pancrazio)* placed on a very high rock reaching into the sea.

1. Aerial view of the archaeological sight

2. The Etruscan Tagliata

3. The rests of the Roman Port

In the background of pictures 2 and 3 notice the "Torre Tagliata"

CAPALBIO

Capalbio is an obviously Medieval town placed on the homonymous hill. In the past it was ruled by the Aldobrandeschis and by the Orsinis, and then it was conquered by the Senese in the first half of the 14th century.

Enclosed by strong walls in which the beautiful *Porta Senese (i.e. Senese Gate)* opens up, it is dominated by the grand *Tower* of the *Rocca degli Aldobrandeschi (i.e. Aldobrandeschi Fortress)* in which we also find the *Collacchioni Palace*. Particularly interesting is the *Pieve di San Nicola (i.e. Parish of San Nicola)* and the nearby *Oratorio della Provvidenza (i.e. Oratory of Providence)* placed immediately outside the town walls.

In September, every year, is the *Sagra del Cinghiale (i.e. Wild Boar Festival)* which has by now become a real gastronomic-cultural tradition.

Separated from the sea by a narrow sandy shore, at the foot of Capalbio is the *Lake of Burano* which, since 1968, on request of the World Wildlife Fund, has become a protected refuge for the permanent and passing-by fauna.

1. Aerial view from the sea: in the foreground the lake of Burano and the Spanish Buranaccia Tower

2. Aerial view of the town

3. View of the Medieval centre

CHIANCIANO TERME

Placed along the sides of the Chiana Valley, the pretty little town of Chianciano Terme is known most of all for its thermal baths, which are particularly suitable for curing liver illnesses. Chianciano Terme is made of an old part, probably of Etruscan origin, placed on a hill and still partly surrounded by ancient walls. Here we find a nice Rocca (i.e. Fortress), the *Palazzo del Podestà* and the *Palazzo dell'Arcipretura* with the *Museo d'Arte Sacra (i.e. Museum of Sacred Art)*. The modern part, placed more towards the valley, is gathered around the four large thermal establishments and is full of gardens and alleys planted with trees.

1. A detail of the thermal baths

2. View of the ancient town

3. The historic centre

4. The city centre

MONTEPULCIANO

Even this town is clearly of Medieval origin. Among the main monuments in Montepulciano we see the 14th century *Palazzo Comunale (i.e. Town-Hall)* attributed to Michelozzo and the *Palazzo Neri Orselli* which contains the *Museo Civico (i.e. Municipal Museum)*. Even the 16th century Cathedral and the *Church of Sant'Agostino* by Michelozzo are beautiful.

1. Aerial view of the historic centre
2. The Church of San Biagio
3. The Cathedral: the Baptismal Font

PIENZA

The lovely little town of Pienza is placed on the top of a hill from which it dominates the Val d'Orcie and the Tresa stream. Its urban system, which is suitable for a much larger town, is due to the will of Pope Pius II Piccolomini who in 1462 changed its ancient name of *Corsignano* into the present name of Pienza.

On the central square rise the *Cathedral,* built towards the end of the 15th century on a project by Rossellino, the *Casa dei Canonici (i.e. House of the Canons),* the seat of the *Museum of the Cathedral*, the *Bishop's Palace* and the *Town-Hall.*

1. *The Town-Hall seen from the Cathedral*
2. *The Cathedral seen from the Town-Hall*
3. *The Diocesan Museum, Duccio da Buoninsegna: Madonna with Child*

133

SAN QUIRICO D' ORCIA

Even San Quirico d'Orcia is an ancient Medieval village which used to be the seat of an Imperial Vicariate. The 12th century *Pieve di San Quirico in Osenna (i.e. Parish of San Quirico in Osenna)*, the P*raetorial Palace* and the *Orti Leonini* (a lovely park with beautiful gardens) are all worth visiting.

1. The Collegiate Church

2. The Parish Church of San Quirico in Osenna

THE ABBEY OF SAN GALGANO

The ruins of the lovely abbey of San Galgano built by the *Cistercian Monks* at the beginning of the 13th century are one of the rare examples of the Gothic-Cistercian style. The Church, which is in the shape of a Latin Cross, is now completely uncovered and the interior is invaded by plants. Of the annexed Monastery remain only some halls and monks' cells as well as the Choir.

Aerial view of the rests of the Abbey

SIENA

The legend says that the beautiful town of Siena, placed on three hills lying between the valleys of the Arbia, the Elsa and the Merse rivers, was founded by Remo's sons Aschio and Senio who came here to seek refuge from their uncle Romolo. Maybe there is some truth in this story, because in the symbol of Siena there is a She-wolf, similar to the one in Rome.

The first certain information, though, states that Siena was a militar colony of Caesar's, called *Sena Julia*. It then came under the domination of the Longobards, of the Carolingians and of the Bishops; finally, at the beginning of the 12th century, it managed to become a *Free City;* the *Consuls* who governed it encouraged it very much towards an urban expansion and trade also by building the *Via Franchigena* which connected Siena to France.

Siena sided with the Ghibellinis and fought some bloody wars againsts Florence (sustained by the Guelfis). In 1260 Siena won the *Battle of Montaperti,* but in 1269 it underwent a final defeat in the *Battle of Colle Val d'Elsa.*

Siena went from times of splendour (with the *Government of the Nine*) to times of darkness (it even underwent the domination of the Germans and Spaniards), but in 1559 it came under the Seignory of Cosimo I de' Medici. In the following centuries it was part of the *Grand Duchy of Tuscany* of the Lorenas, and then, in 1859 it was the first Tuscan town to belong to the Kingdom of Italy.

1. Night view

2. A view of Piazza del Campo

On pages 136-137

1-2-3. Spectacular views of Piazza del Campo

4. The Fonte Gaia

1

2

136

3

4

PIAZZA DEL CAMPO AND PALAZZO PUBBLICO

Piazza del Campo is the heart of town and it is unique in the world for its shape. It has a gradient because it was built at the confluence of the three hills on which the town rises; it is in the shape of a shell and its beautiful brick floor is divided into nine segments starting from the *Palazzo Pubblico,* which was almost for sure devoted to the *Government of the Nine.* In the lower part, dominated by the imposing *Torre del Mangia (i.e. Mangia Tower)* we find the *Palazzo Pubblico* built between the 13th and the 14th century, seat of the Municipality and of the Municipal Museum. The façade is decorated with beautiful windows with three lights; inside are many halls, all frescoed by local artists, who in that time founded the *Scuola Senese (i.e. Senese School)* and left works of inestimable artistic value.

On the first floor we find the *Municipal Museum* containing some of the most precious artistic collections of Tuscany. Among the numerous halls, we recall the *Sala del Mappamondo (i.e. Hall of the Globe)* in which we can admire two masterpieces by Simone Martini: the *Maestà (i.e. Majesty)* and *Guidariccio da Fogliano.*

Opposite the Palazzo Pubblico, in the highest part of the square, we find the beautiful *Fonte Gaia* decorated with lovely copies of the reliefs engraved by the local artist Jacopo della Quercia; the originals are kept in the Palazzo Pubblico.

1. The Palazzo Pubblico:
the Renaissance Hall

2. The Municipal Museum: the Balia hall
with frescos by Spinello Aretino

3. *The Chapel*

4. The Chapel: Taddeo di Bartolo,
frescos with stories about the Madonna

5. The Globe hall: Simone Martini,
Guidoriccio da Fogliano

4

5

THE PALIO

We cannot talk about Siena without mentioning the *Palio* which takes place twice a year (on July 2nd and on August 16th) in Piazza del Campo; during the race 10 horses are ridden bareback by the representatives of 10 of the 17 *Contrade* in which the town is divided. The race takes place all around the perimetre of *Piazza del Campo* and every year thousands of spectators come to watch the show from the centre of the square and from the windows of the houses all around.

The Palio is the real expression of rivalry dividing the inhabitants of the various Contrade and it is preceded and followed by long celebrations starting with the drawing of the contrade and of the horses, who are then blessed with their riders in the Churches of the various city quarters.

The race dates back to the first half of the 15th century; it starts in the morning with the blessing of the contrade flags and of the Palio itself in the *Church of Santa Maria del Provenzano* on July 2nd, and in the Cathedral on August 16th. In the afternoon the historic parade starts, which is led by the *Mazzieri* of the Municipality, followed by the *Centurioni*, by the representatives of the contrade, and finally by the oxen hauled *Carroccio* on which is the *Palio (i.e. Prize)* offered to the winner. After this come the 10 horses, who are lined up along the scratch line made of a rope called *Canapo (Hemp)*. When the bell in the Torre del Mangia starts striking, the Canapo is dropped and the race starts; the horses have to ride round the piazza three times in little more than one minute.

1. The "Carroccio" (i.e. Cart) carrying the Palio (i.e. Prize)

2. The blessing of the rider and of the horse

3. The start

4. The public crowding the Piazza

3

4

THE CATHEDRAL

The building of this beautiful Church lasted longer than two centuries, from 1150 to 1376, because the works were interrupted various times for the wars which opposed Siena to Florence; the citizens of Siena decided to make the Cathedral larger than the one in Florence, but they failed in their attempt for static reasons. For the fact of being built over such a long period of time, it presents various styles, from the Romanesque to the Gothic and the Flowery Gothic.

The lower part of the pink and green marble façade was built by Giovanni Pisano, whereas the upper part was completed by Giovanni di Cecco. See the big central rose-window with its glass window representing the *Last Supper,* surrounded by 40 busts representing the four Evangelists and 36 Patriarchs and Prophets. Even the floor is beautiful with its 56 panels made by different artists; it is uncovered every year only between August 15th and September 15th.

The interior contains many works of art, among which we remember a most beautiful glass window designed by Duccio di Boninsegna, statues by Michelangelo, Bernini, Donatello, Pinturicchio and Jacopo della Quercia.

The lovely Pulpit was made by Nicola Pisano with the help of his son Giovanni and of Arnolfo di Cambio. It has an octagonal base and it is sustained by nine columns. The lovely parapet panels represent the *Stories of Christ* and are separated by images of Prophets and Angels.

The tall Bell-Tower built at the beginning of the 14th century on a project by Giovanni and Agnolo di Ventura, is particular for its black and white stripes and for the six windows on each side, starting from the bottom with windows with one light and increasing to windows with six lights.

1. The Cathedral

2. The churchyard and the portals on the façade

THE BAPTISTERY

Obtained from extending the Cathedral Choir, the Baptistery was built between 1317 and 1325, in the same style as the Cathedral itself. Inside it is divided into three aisles with pointed vaults. In the centre rises a real masterpiece of Early Renaissance art: the *Baptismal Font* which is composed of a hexagonal basin with a bronze panel on each side, created by Donatello, Ghiberti and Jacopo della Quercia. The latter also made the lovely hexagonal *Ciborium*.

1. The Baptistery
2. The Baptistery: the Baptismal Font
3. The Cathedral: the Pulpit by Nicola Pisano
4. The Cathedral: the central aisle

3

1

2

4

THE MUSEUM OF THE CATHEDRAL

In the Museum of the Cathedral we find many sculptures, paintings, masterpieces of the art of working gold, as well as miniatures, ornaments and tapestries, most of which deriving from the Cathedral. This Museum is composed of various halls placed on different floors, but even the walls along the corridors and stairs are all covered with works of art.

1. Duccio da Buoninsegna: the Great Majesty

2. Pietro Lorenzetti: Nativity of Mary (detail)

3. Spectacular aerial view of the historic centre

144

THE NATIONAL PICTURE-GALLERY

Placed in the Gothic *Palazzo Buonsignori* (15th century), the *Pinacoteca Nazionale (i.e. National Picture-Gallery)* was founded in 1932 to reorder and complete precedent collections. It is an almost complete collection of the Senese painting from the end of the 12th to the 18th century.

The Picture-Gallery is on the first floor of the building and it is composed of about 40 halls in which the works of art are exposed in chronological order.

1. Hall 17 with works by Sano di Pietro
2. Simone Martini: Madonna with Child
3. Palazzo Buonsignori, the seat of the Museum

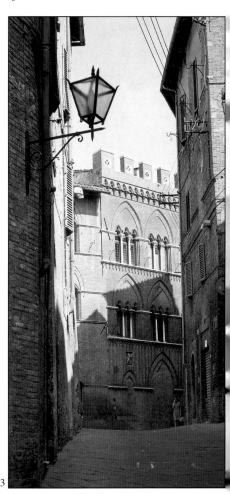

146

Siena is famous for being the seat of one of the most ancient banks in the world, the *Monte dei Paschi,* and also for being the place of birth of Santa Caterina, Italy's Patron Saint.

The 13th-14th century Church of *San Domenico* contains the famous *Chapel of Santa Caterina* which is richly frescoed by Sodoma. The Church of *Santa Caterina* contains lovely Oratories and the Saint's cell.

1. Andrea Vanni: Portrait of Santa Caterina (detail)

2. Aerial view of the Basilica of San Domenico: the Fonte Branda to the right

3. The Tolomei Palace

4. Via Santa Caterina with the house where the Saint was born

5. The Monte dei Paschi building

1

POGGIBONSI

Today Poggibonsi is the most important industrial town of the region around Siena, and it is also a historic town for many bloody wars between the Senese and Florentines were fought here.

Do not miss to see the *Palazzo Pretorio (i.e. Praetorial Palace)* in Gothic style; its façade is decorated with coats-of-arms and flanked by an imposing tower as well as the *Collegiata (i.e. Collegiate Church)* and the *Church of San Lorenzo* containing lovely works of art.

1. *Piazza Cavour*
2. *The Badia Castle*
3. *The San Lucchese Basilica*
4. *The Collegiate Church*
5. *The Strozzavolpe Castle*

2

4

3

5

MONTERIGGIONI

The tiny Medieval village of Monteriggioni was built by the Senese at the beginning of the 13th century as a defence outpost against the attacks of the Florentines. For this reason, in fact, it has the aspect of a fortress and it is completely surrounded by 14 towers and strong walls. Inside the walls rises a pretty *Parish* in Romanesque-Gothic style.

1. Aerial view

2. One of the gates

149

SAN GIMIGNANO

Placed on the top of a hill dominating the Elsa Valley, this lovely town of evident Medieval origin is renowned for its numerous *Towers* gathered in the historic centre and very close to one another. Today there are only 14 of the original 72 towers. Although San Giminiano is of Etruscan origin, it started to develop only around the 12th century when the famous *Via Franchigena* was built nearby.

The historic centre, still surrounded by strong walls, has its heart in a huge 13th century tank placed among the Medieval palaces and dominated by the *Torri Guelfe Gemelle (i.e. Twin Guelfi Towers)* and by the *Torre del Diavolo (i.e. Devil's Tower)* annexed to the *Palazzo Cortesi*.

Notice the lovely *Piazza Duomo (i.e. Cathedral Square)* on which rises the Romanesque *Collegiata* (or Cathedral) built in the 13th century on the ramains of the ancient *Parish of San Giminiano*.

1-3. Aerial views

2. The Cathedral or Collegiate Church of Santa Maria Assunta

4. Inside the Cathedral

3

The inside is divided into three aisles and it contains precious frescoes and works by the main local artists from that period. The square is dominated by the *Torre Rognosa (i.e. Rognosa Tower)* dominating over the *Palazzo del Podestà*.
Opposite this building rises the *Palazzo Pretorio (i.e. Praetorial Palace)* containing the *Museo Civico (i.e. Municipal Museum)* in which many precious 13th and 14th century works of local and Florentine artists are kept. Also see the imposing pentagonal *Rocca (i.e. Fortress)* built by the Florentines in the middle of the 14th century.

4

1

2

3

152

1. *View of the Towers*

2. *The Arco dei Belli, on the first circle of walls*

3-4. *Piazza della Cisterna (i.e the Piazza of the Tank)*

5. *Piazza del Duomo with the Palazzo del Podestà and the Torre Rognosa*

6. *The courtyard inside the Town-Hall*

4

5

6

AREZZO

Placed on a hill dominating the valleys of the Arno, Tiber and Chiana rivers, Arezzo is a very ancient town, one of the most important *Lucumons* of the Etruscan *Dodecapoli.* The town is still surrounded by the strong walls of the time. Having passed under the domination of the Roman Empire, in the 1st century bC it became a *Municipio;* in that period, the art of working gold (which still today makes Arezzo famous around the world) was encouraged and developed.

After having gone through the domination of the Longobards, the Franks and the Marquis of Tuscany, Arezzo became a *Free City* in the 11th century. In the following centuries Arezzo, who by then had become very strong, competed with Florence for the control over the territory; but in 1289 Arezzo was decisively defeated in the *Battle of Campaldino* therefore becoming part of the Grand Duchy of Tuscany, first under the Medicis and then under the Lorenas. Finally, in 1860 it became part of the Kingdom of Italy.

Arezzo is the birthplace of Francesco Petrarca, the great Poet. The house he was born in in 1304 has now become the seat of the Academy devoted to him.

1. Aerial view of town

2. The Praetorial Palace

PIAZZA DUOMO

In the highest part of town we find *Piazza Duomo,* dominated by the grandness of the Gothic style Cathedral, whose building started in 1278 on a project by the architect Margaritone, but it was only finished in the first years of the 16th century, therefore there are some evident differences in style. Polystyle columns divide the Cathedral into three aisles; inside it contains many precious works among which is the famous fresco *La Maddalena* made in 1465 by Pier della Francesca.

Not very far away, overlooking the homonymous square, rises the *Basilica of San Francesco* in Gothic style with Umbrian-Franciscan influence. The Basilica was built between the 13th and the 15th century with a very simple brick façade; the walls inside (in the single nave), though, are all enriched with frescoes among which is the beautiful cycle of the *Trionfi della Croce (i.e. Triumphs of the Cross),* one of Pier della Francesca's principal works.

Not far from here we find the *Fortezza Medicea (i.e. Medici Fortress),* a strong fortification with a star-shaped plan, built in the 16th century.

1. The Tower and part of the apse

2. Aerial view of the Cathedral: on the background, in the garden, rises the monument to Francesco Petrarca

3. The Church of San Francesco: the Annunciation of Mary (detail)

4. The Town-Hall

PIAZZA GRANDE

Piazza Grande is typical for its irregular planimetry. On the left hand side rises the lovely apse of the adjoining *Pieve di Santa Maria (i.e. Parish Church of Santa Maria)*, a masterpiece of Romanesque art, built between 1140 and 1300; its façade has four arches, whereas the inside is divided into three aisles where, among other works, we can see a lovely *Polyptich* made by Pietro Lorenzetti in 1320. On Piazza Grande also rise the *Palazzo delle Logge (i.e. Palace of the Loggias)* built in the 16th century on a design by Vasari, the *Palazzo della Fraternità dei Laici (i.e. Palace of the Laymen Brotherhood)* by Rossellino, the Medieval *Torre dei Lappoli* and *Torre Faggiolana* facing each other.

Do not miss to see the nearby 14th-15th century *Palazzo Pretorio (i.e. Praetorial Palace)*, the *Palazzo dei Priori* (or *Comunale*) and the *Vasari House* which has become the seat of the *Vasari Archive*. See the lovely *Church of San Domenico* with its 13th-14th century Bell-Tower built in Gothic style, whose inside walls were frescoed by Spinello Aretino; there is also a lovely Crucifix by Cimabue dominating over the Main Altar. Outside the 15th century Church of *Santa Maria delle Grazie* is a beautiful porch by Benedetto da Maiano, whereas inside is a lovely marble and terracotta statue by Andrea della Robbia. Do not forget to visit the *Museo Archeologico (i.e. Archaeological Museum)* full of the many Etruscan and Roman ruins found in this area; the Museum overlooks the few ruins of the *Anfiteatro Romano (i.e. Roman Anfitheatre)* built in the shape of an ellipse with two rows of steps from the 1st-2nd century.

1. *Aerial view*

2. *Aerial view: Pieve di Santa Maria in the foreground*

3. *The Church of San Domenico: the façade*

4. *The Church of San Domenico: the sobre inside with the frescos by Spinello Aretino and the Crucifix by Cimabue over the altar*

5. *The Roman Anfitheatre and the Archaeological Museum*

6. *The beautiful porch outside the Church of Santa Maria delle Grazie*

THE SARACEN JOUST

The Saracen Joust takes place in Piazza Grande every year on the first Sunday in September. The competition, which is preceded by a show of the famous *Sbandieratori (i.e. Flag-wavers)* and by a parade of the representatives of the four town quarters in historic costume, consists in hitting a shield with a spear after a crazy gallop; the shield is sustained by one of the arms of the *Saracino (i.e. Saracen)*; the difficulty of the race consists in the fact that this has to be done without being hurt by the mace hanging on the other arm; when the shield is hit by the rider's spear, the Saracen starts turning quickly. The winner is whoever manages to hit the shield the greatest number of times without being hit by the mace.

1. The "Sbandieratori" (i.e Flag-wavers)

2. The representatives of the different town quarters

3. the "Saracen" seen from the back

CORTONA

Surrounded by strong *Etruscan Walls* and dominated by the *Fortezza Medicea del Girifalco (i.e. Girifalco Fortress of the Medicis)*, Cortona is placed on a steep hill at the confluence of the Tiber and Chiana valleys. Cortona's urban system is typically Medieval, and so are also the most important town monuments, among which we recall the 13th century *Palazzo Comunale (i.e. Town-Hall)*, the *Palazzo Pretorio (i.e. Praetorial Palace)* contain-ing the *Museo dell'Accademia Etrusca (i.e. Etruscan Academy Museum)* with its ruins, the 13th century *Church of San Francesco,* the 15th century *Church of San Domenico* and the *Cathedral* built by Giuliano da Sangallo on the ruins of the existing Church of Santa Maria.

1. Aerial view: on the peak rises the Girifalco fortress
2. The Town Hall
3. The Etruscan Tomb at Ipogeo called "Tamella di Pitagora"

CONTENTS

© Copyright 2005 by
Officina Grafica Bolognese s.r.l.
Via del Fonditore, 6/5 - 40138 Bologna - Italy
Tel. +39 051.53.22.03 - Fax +39 051.53.21.88 - E-mail: ogb@tuttopmi.it

Printed in UE
by Officina Grafica Bolognese s.r.l. - Bologna - Italy

Text and paging by O.G.B.

Pictures by: M. Agnoletto, L. Angeli, V. Bellucci,
Comm. Giambruni, Santori sas, Foto Gielle, N. Grifoni, G. Orlandi

Translation: Benedict School (Vanessa Pasquali)